MARTIN HEIDEGGER, before his retirement, was professor of philosophy at the University of Frieburg. He is a foremost existential twentieth-century philosopher.

PS

HEIDEGGER, Martin. Identity and Difference, tr. with an intro. by J. Stambaugh. bilingual ed. Harper & Row, 1969. 146p 69-17025. 5.00

CHOICE   FEB. '70
Philosophy

This short volume contains two recent lectures of Martin Heidegger, Germany's greatest thinker of the present. They are "The Principle of Identity" and "The Onto-theo-logical Constitution of Metaphysics." Heidegger himself regards this book as one of his most important, since it marks the start of the most recent phase of his still developing thought. Excellently translated and introduced by Joan Stambaugh, it is the latest in the Harper and Row series of Heidegger works, done in close collaboration with the author. Necessary for all libraries and for serious students of Heidegger.

MARTIN HEIDEGGER
WORKS

General Editor J. Glenn Gray
Colorado College

———

Also by Martin Heidegger
BEING AND TIME

DISCOURSE ON THINKING
(*Gelassenheit*)

WHAT IS CALLED THINKING?
(*Was heisst Denken?*)

MARTIN HEIDEGGER

IDENTITY AND DIFFERENCE

Translated

and

with an Introduction by

JOAN STAMBAUGH

1817

HARPER & ROW, PUBLISHERS

NEW YORK, EVANSTON, AND LONDON

Originally published by Verlag Günther Neske in Pfullingen under the title *Identität und Differenz.* Copyright 1957 by Verlag Günther Neske in Pfullingen.

English translation by Joan Stambaugh.

IDENTITY AND DIFFERENCE. *Copyright © 1969 in the English translation by Harper & Row, Publishers, Incorporated, New York.*

FIRST EDITION

LIBRARY OF CONGRESS CATALOG CARD NUMBER: 69-17025

CONTENTS

IDENTITY AND DIFFERENCE

INTRODUCTION

by JOAN STAMBAUGH

The problem of identity has been a basic philosophical issue since Parmenides. Parmenides stated it in the form: "thought and being are the same," with a radicality and a simplicity perhaps never again possible for later thinkers. Heidegger has pondered over Parmenides' statement for years, returning to it again and again in his writings. Thus it came as no surprise to this translator when Heidegger stated that he considered *Identity and Difference* to be the most important thing he has published since *Being and Time*.

That is quite a statement. For between *Being and Time* and *Identity and Difference* lies a veritable wealth of publications throwing light upon the problem of Being and wrestling with the historical oblivion of that problem. The oblivion of Being is not something omitted in the history of philosophy, something left out. Metaphysics has asked the question of Being, but only to bring Being into a relationship with beings as their *ground*.

Identity and Difference shares with *Being and Time* the fundamental problem of the relation of man and Being. But whereas in
Being and Time Heidegger began with an analysis of the meaning
of man (*Dasein*), proceeding from there toward an understanding
of Being, *Identity and Difference* asks about that very "relation"
itself *as* the relation of man and Being. It does not inquire into the
"components" of the relation, but into the relation as a relation.
This manner of thinking about the problem of identity sets Heidegger apart from the traditional metaphysical consideration of that
problem. It brings him closer to the pre-metaphysical thinker
Parmenides' dimension of identity. As Heidegger points out, Parmenides thinks Being from the point of view of identity as a
characteristic of this identity. But later, Metaphysics comes to represent identity as a characteristic of Being. Thus the originality
native to identity as thought by Parmenides became subservient to
the metaphysical understanding of Being.

In the history of Western philosophy, identity was at first
thought as unity, as the unity of a thing with itself. The two thinkers who were most explicitly concerned with unity or identity as a
central problem were perhaps Plotinus and Leibniz. Plotinus begins
his sixth Ennead, 9 with the statement: "It is in virtue of unity that
beings are beings." Plotinus' ultimate reality, the One, is beyond
even Being, a statement that puts Plotinus on the borderline of

8

Western thought. Leibniz develops the concept of unity in his Monadology as simplicity, individuality and, above all, uniqueness which he establishes with the help of the principle of the identity of indiscernibles. (If two things have absolutely nothing which distinguishes them from each other, they are identical, they are the same thing.)

One thinker who was concerned with the problem of identity as such was Nicholas of Cusa. The dimension in which he thought the problem of identity was not that of the unity of beings, but the relation of God to the world, of the infinite to the finite. His first formulation of the problem was the *coincidentia oppositorum,* the coincidence of opposites. But even more interesting is his later formulation: The non-other is none other than the non-other. Cusanus can define anything with reference to its self-identity and its negation of otherness. But the "non-other" itself by its definition admits of no difference, no otherness whatsoever. Its very nature is to be non-other. Thus Cusanus succeeds in formulating God as the Non-other, as nothing other than himself and as nothing other than the world.

As Heidegger remarks, it took philosophy two thousand years to formulate the problem of identity in its fully developed form as mediation and synthesis. With Leibniz and Kant preparing the way, the German Idealists Fichte, Hegel, and Schelling place identity in the center of their thought on the foundation of transcendental reflection. These thinkers are concerned not with the simple unity of a thing with itself, but with the mediated syntheses of subject and object, of subjectivity and objectivity as such. If one put Parmenides' statement "Thought and Being are the same" in the context of German Idealism, one would get a statement something like: Being is thought, i.e., all "Being" is ultimately thought, the absolute Idea (Hegel), and is destined to become thought. Whatever Being there might be outside thought is simply not yet thought, not yet mediated in the absolute synthesizing activity of the Idea. The simplest statement of this can be found in the Preface to Hegel's *Philosophy of Law*: "The real is the rational and the rational is the real." The principle of identity $A = A$ becomes reformulated by Fichte as $I = I$, and by Schelling's Philosophy of Identity as the identity, more precisely as the indifference of subject and object. It is perhaps Schelling who in his own way, and still basically although not totally within the framework of Idealism, comes closest to Heidegger's dimension of the problem of identity when he states in *Of Human Freedom* that there must be a being *before* all basis (ground) and before all existence, before any duality at all. Since this being precedes all antitheses, it cannot constitute their identity; it can only be the absolute in-difference of both. Indifference is not a product of antitheses, nor are antitheses implicitly contained in it. It is far rather a unique being apart from all antitheses. It is the groundless. With his idea of the groundless, Schelling is closer to the dimension of Heidegger's thinking than to German Idealism. Yet he still calls this groundless "a being."

How does Heidegger treat the problem of identity and in what dimension does this problem now lie if no longer within the framework of metaphysics as the problem of the unity of a thing with itself or as the transcendentally mediated unity of absolute reflection? Heidegger conceives the problem of identity in such a fundamental way that what is "identical," Being and man, can only be thought from the nature of identity itself. He begins his exposition by questioning the principle of identity as a principle of thinking. He concludes that the principle of identity presupposes the meaning of identity itself. A principle of thought must also be a principle of Being (this "also" is, of course, misleading), the principle: to every being as such there belongs identity, the unity with itself. This is a fundamental characteristic of the Being of beings.

Heidegger then questions Parmenides' statement that thought and Being are the same, interpreting that statement to mean: Being belongs—together with thought—into the Same. A = A has become A *is* (transitively) A, and the "is" now takes on the meaning of belonging together. Heidegger understands the "is" in identity as the relation of belonging together, and it is this new meaning of identity which concerns him in this lecture. What is new about this understanding of identity as a relation is that the relation first determines the manner of being of what is to be related and the how of this relation. It is perhaps difficult for us to think of a relation as being more original than what is related, but this is what Heidegger requires of us. This relation is then no relation in the ordinary sense of that term. We do not know and we cannot predict what is related. Man does not have the static essence of the animal rationale or the subject thinking its object. One of Heidegger's most basic insights is that we do not know what man is, even if he could be understood as a "what" at all. To say that an understanding of Being is "subjective" because man is involved in that understanding is simply thoughtless. Man is, in the language of *Being and Time*, Being-there (*Da-Sein*), man is the "there" of Being. This has nothing to do with subjectivity and nothing to do with the concept of human existence of "existentialism."

Identity is belonging-together. If the element of *together* in belonging-together is emphasized, we have the metaphysical concept of identity which orders the manifold into a unity mediated by synthesis. This unity forms a systematic totality of the world with God or Being as the ground, as the first cause and as the highest being. But if the element of *belonging* in belonging together is emphasized, we have thinking and Being held apart and at the same time held together (not fitted together) in the Same. To come closer to an understanding of the *belonging* together of man and Being, we must leave metaphysical thinking which thinks Being exclusively as the cause of beings and thinks beings primarily as what is caused. But we cannot leave metaphysics by a series of reasoned conclusions. We must simply leap out of it. Thus the principle (*Satz*) of identity becomes a leap (*Satz*) out of metaphysics.

This brings Heidegger to the form of *belonging* together of man and Being in our present age of technology. A short comment might be inserted here about Heidegger's emphasis on thinking as that which man is. One might ask: isn't man more than thought, doesn't he also have emotions, needs as to how he lives, practical problems, etc.? Isn't Heidegger's understanding of man too rationalistic, too idealistic in its emphasis on thought? To this question it must be answered: all of these aspects of man are included in what Heidegger calls thinking. Thinking is not the "upper story" of the split-level being that is the rational animal. Thinking in the form of the Logos has, for instance, brought about the whole world of technology and the atomic age which is concrete enough. Technology isn't just something man has acquired as an accessory. Right now it is what he *is*.

"Technology" is nothing technical. It is not even a "product" of man. The manner in which man and Being concern each other in the world of technology Heidegger calls the framework. The framework is far more real than all atomic energy and all machines. But it is nothing necessarily ultimate. It could be a prelude to what Heidegger calls the event of appropriation.[1] The event of appropriation is the realm in which man and Being reach each other in their very core. They lose the determinations placed upon them by metaphysics.

Metaphysics thinks identity as a fundamental trait of Being. For Heidegger, Being and thought belong to an identity whose acting nature stems from the letting *belong* together which is called the event of appropriation. It took thinking two thousand years to arrive at an understanding of identity as transcendentally mediated identity. We cannot expect to grasp instantly the meaning of the

---

[1] Framework or Frame (*Ge-Stell*) and event of appropriation (*Er-eignis*) are perhaps the two key words in this lecture. They are extremely difficult to translate. "*Ge-Stell*" in the sense in which Heidegger uses it does not belong to common language. In German, "*Berg*" means a mountain, "*Gebirge*" means a chain or group of mountains. In the same way "*Ge-Stell*" is the unity (but *not* a unity in the sense of a general whole subsuming all particulars under it) of all the activities in which the verb "*stellen*" (place, put, set) figures: *vor-stellen* (represent, think), *stellen* (challenge), *ent-stellen* (disfigure), *nach-stellen* (to be after someone, pursue him stealthily), *sicher-stellen* (to make certain of something).

The event of appropriation (*Ereignis*) is a word belonging to common language and means "event." But Heidegger's use of it is more (1) "abstract" in the sense of being infinitely removed from everyday events and yet of being that which is so close to us that we cannot see it, and (2) "concrete" in its use of the very *roots* of that word: *er-eignen* (*eigen*=own, thus to come into one's own, to come to where one *belongs*) and *er-äugnen* (*Auge*=eye. This is the real etymological root of er-eignen), thus to catch sight of, to see with the mind's eye, to see face-to-face.

14

non-metaphysical identity Heidegger shows us here.

The Onto-theo-logical Constitution of Metaphysics is a lecture given at the end of a Hegel seminar. Whereas *Identity and Difference* looks ahead, the *Onto-theo-logical Constitution of Metaphysics* looks back at the realm of the essential origin of metaphysics.

Metaphysical thinking is determined by the difference between Being and beings. The way in which metaphysics has thought the relation of Being and beings has given it the structure of both ontology and theology, regardless of whether it has made explicit use of these terms or not. Metaphysics is ontology in that it thinks Being as the first and most universal ground common to all beings. Metaphysics is theology in that it thinks Being as the highest ground above all beings, ultimately as the ground of itself, *causa sui*, which is the metaphysical concept of God. Metaphysics is thus in its very nature onto-theo-logic.

Heidegger begins with the question: What is thinking concerned with?, and compares his own answer to this question with that of Hegel. For both Hegel and Heidegger, thought is concerned with Being. But for Hegel Being is absolute thought thinking itself. How does Being come to manifest itself as absolute thought for Hegel? Since the beginning of metaphysics, Being has shown itself as having the character of ground, of Logos. Thus thinking has concentrated on finding Being as the ground, on giving reasons (*ratio*)

15

in answer to the question "why?" In the epochal clearing of Being reached with Hegel, Being has become the absolute concept grasping itself, the "absolute" has become the absolute *Idea*. This absolute Idea moves forward through history toward the absolute, total result of history in which all individual distinctions are at once negated as being merely individual, preserved in their essential being, and elevated into the higher reality of the whole.

For Heidegger, however, thinking is concerned with Being in regard to its difference from beings. Heidegger doesn't ask about Being as the ground of beings; he goes from what is as yet unthought, from the difference between Being and beings *as difference* (the ontological difference), to that which is to be thought, the *oblivion* of that difference. The difference is nothing that man has somehow "forgotten." Oblivion belongs intrinsically to difference.

Instead of progressing toward an all-inclusive totality, thinking for Heidegger attempts to move *forward* by the step *back* into the realm of the essence of truth which has never yet come to light. This step back allows Being as difference to come before thinking without being its object. The step back, which is actually a direction and a manner of thinking and not an isolated step of thought, leads out of metaphysics into the essential origin of metaphysics.

Metaphysics does not heed the ontological difference *as* difference. It looks at the different *elements* of that difference. It sees the difference between Being and beings, but it is concerned primarily with Being as the *ground* of beings and thus never sees the difference as difference. Heidegger characterizes this difference as the difference between Overwhelming and Arrival.[2] The difference grants a "Between" in which the Overwhelming of Being and the arrival in beings are held toward each other and yet held apart. This Between is perdurance.[3] In the perdurance of the difference of Overwhelming and Arrival reigns clearing. In a conversation about the meaning of clearing, Heidegger stated that clearing is the (non-metaphysical) presupposition for revealing and securing. It is the most fundamental presupposition for anything to be or to happen at all.

Toward the end of this lecture Heidegger raises an extremely interesting question: might not this difference somehow belong to the destiny of Being from its very beginning until its completion? The difficulty in affirming this would lie in determining how the difference always belongs to the destiny of Being. It cannot be thought

[2] Overwhelming (*Überkommnis*) is the manner in which Being reaches beings. It preserves the meaning of sur-prise (over-taking) and thus of incalculability. Arrival (*Ankunft*) is, so to speak, the "place" (in beings) in which Being arrives.

[3] (*Austrag*), literally carrying out, holding out. In a consultation Heidegger pointed out the relationship of this word to man as "the stand-in of nothingness" (*What is Metaphysics?*). He stated that its basic meaning is to bear, to hold out, but without any connotation of suffering or exertion. The *Austrag* is the carrying out of the "relation" of Being and beings, endured with an intensity that never lets up.

17

as a general trait always present in the individual epochs of the destiny of Being. Nor can it be thought as a law developing in a dialectical process. The problem here is that the concepts of metaphysics: Being—beings, ground—what is grounded, are no longer adequate to express the thinking which takes place in the realm reached by the step back. These concepts name what is different, they are unable to name the difference itself. Heidegger leaves us with the question: do our Western languages have an intrinsic metaphysical structure so that they are forever destined to be onto-theo-logical in their nature or do they harbor other possibilities of thinking?

18

The Principle of Identity is the unchanged text of a lecture given on the occasion of the 500th anniversary of the University of Freiburg im Breisgau, for the faculty day on June 27, 1957.

The Onto-theo-logical Constitution of Metaphysics is the explication that concluded a seminar during the winter semester 1956-57 on Hegel's *Science of Logic*. It has in part been revised. The lecture took place on February 24, 1957 in Todtnauberg.

The Principle of Identity glances ahead and backward, too; ahead into the realm from which stems the subject matter of the lecture *The Thing* (see notes) ; back to the realm where the essence of metaphysics has its source; the constitution of metaphysics is defined by *difference*.

The close relation of *identity and difference* will be shown in this publication to be that which gives us thought.

The reader is to discover for himself in what way difference stems from the essence of identity, by listening to the harmony presiding over *the event of appropriation* and *perdurance.*

In this realm one cannot prove anything, but one can point out a great deal.

Todtnauberg

September 9, 1957

The usual formulation of the principle of identity reads: A = A. The principle of identity is considered the highest principle of thought. We shall try to think about this principle for a while. For we should like to find out through this principle what identity is.

When thinking attempts to pursue something that has claimed its attention, it may happen that on the way it undergoes a change. It is advisable, therefore, in what follows to pay attention to the path of thought rather than to its content. To dwell properly upon the content would simply block the progress of the lecture.

What does the formula A = A state which is customarily used to represent the principle of identity? The formula expresses the equality of A and A. An equation requires at least two elements. One A is equal to another. Is this what the principle of identity is supposed to mean? Obviously not. That which is identical, in Latin "idem," is in Greek τὸ αὐτό. Translated, τὸ αὐτό means "the same." If someone constantly repeats himself, for example: "the plant is a plant," he speaks in a tautology. For something to be the same, one is always enough. Two are not needed, as they are in the case of equality.

The formula A = A speaks of equality. It doesn't define A as the same. The common formulation of the principle of identity thus conceals precisely what the principle is trying to say: A is A, that is, every A is itself the same.

While we are circumscribing in this fashion what is identical, we are reminded of an old word by which Plato makes the identical perceptible, a word that points back to a still older word. In the dialogue *The Sophist*, 254d, Plato speaks of στάσις and κίνησις, rest and motion. Plato has the stranger say at this point: οὐκοῦν αὐτῶν ἕκαστον τοῖν μὲν δυοῖν ἕτερόν ἐστιν, αὐτὸ δ'ἑαυτῷ ταὐτόν.

"Each one of them is different from the (other) two, but itself the same for itself." Plato doesn't just say: ἕκαστον αὐτὸ ταὐτόν, "each itself the same," but says ἕκαστον ἑαυτῷ ταὐτόν, "each itself the same for itself."

The dative ἑαυτῷ means: each thing itself is returned to itself, each itself is the same for itself with itself. Our language, like the Greek, offers the advantage of making clear with one and the same word what is identical and again clarifying that word in the unity of all its various forms.

The more fitting formulation of the principle of identity "A = A" would accordingly mean not only that every A is itself the same; but rather that every A is itself the same with itself. Sameness implies the relation of "with," that is, a mediation, a connection, a synthesis: the unification into a unity. This is why throughout the history of Western thought identity appears as unity. But that unity is by no means the stale emptiness of that which, in itself without relation, persists in monotony. However, to get to the point where the relationship of the same with itself—which prevails in that identity which was already implicitly present very early—emerges as this mediation in a decisive and characteristic way, and where an abode is found for this radiant emergence, of mediation within identity, Western thought required more than two thousand years. For it is only the philosophy of speculative Idealism, prepared by Leibniz and Kant, that through Fichte, Schelling, and Hegel established an abode for the essence, in itself synthetic, of identity. This abode cannot be demonstrated here. Just one thing we must keep in mind: since the era of speculative Idealism, it is no longer possible for thinking to represent the unity of identity as mere sameness, and to disregard the mediation that prevails in unity. Wherever this is done, identity is represented only in an abstract manner.

Even in the improved formula "A is A," abstract identity alone appears. Does it get that far? Does the principle of identity really

25

say anything about the nature of identity? No, at least not directly. Rather, the principle already presupposes what identity means and where it belongs. How do we get any information about this presupposition? The principle of identity itself gives it to us, if we listen carefully to its key note, if we think about that key note instead of just thoughtlessly mouthing the formula "A is A." For the proposition really says: "A *is* A." What do we hear? With this "is," the principle tells us how every being is, namely: it itself is the same with itself. The principle of identity speaks of the Being of beings. As a law of thought, the principle is valid only insofar as it is a principle of Being that reads: To every being as such there belongs identity, the unity with itself.

What the principle of identity, heard in its fundamental key, states is exactly what the whole of Western European thinking has in mind—and that is: the unity of identity forms a basic characteristic in the Being of beings. Everywhere, wherever and however we are related to beings of every kind, we find identity making its claim on us. If this claim were not made, beings could never appear in their Being. Accordingly, there would then also not be any science. For if science could not be sure in advance of the identity of its object in each case, it could not be what it is. By this assurance, research makes certain that its work is possible. Still, the leading idea of the identity of the object is never of any palpable use to the sciences. Thus, what is successful and fruitful about scientific knowledge is everywhere based on something useless. The claim of the identity of the object *speaks*, whether the sciences hear it or not, whether they throw to the winds what they have heard or let themselves be strongly affected by it.

The claim of identity speaks from the Being of beings. However, where the Being of beings appears, most early and most authentically in Western thought—with Parmenides—there speaks τὸ αὐτό, that which is identical, in a way that is almost too powerful. One of Parmenides' fragments reads: τὸ γὰρ αὐτὸ νοεῖν ἐστίν τε καὶ εἶναι.

"For the same perceiving (thinking) as well as being."

Different things, thinking and Being, are here thought of as the Same. What does this say? It says something wholly different from what we know otherwise as the doctrine of metaphysics, which states that identity belongs to Being. Parmenides says: Being belongs to an identity. What does identity mean here? What does the word τὸ αὐτό, the Same, say in Parmenides' fragment? Parmenides gives us no answer. He places us before an enigma which we may not sidestep. We must acknowledge the fact that in the earliest period of thinking, long before thinking had arrived at a principle of identity, identity itself speaks out in a pronouncement which rules as follows: thinking and Being belong together in the Same and by virtue of this Same.

Unintentionally we have here already interpreted τὸ αὐτό,

the Same. We interpret Sameness to mean a belonging together. The obvious thing to do would be to represent this belonging together in the sense of identity as it was thought and generally understood later on. What could prevent us? None other than the principle itself which we read in Parmenides. For it says something else—it says that Being, together with thinking, belongs in the Same. Being is determined by an identity as a characteristic of that identity. Later on, however, identity as it is thought of in metaphysics is represented as a characteristic of Being. Thus we must not try to determine the identity that Parmenides speaks of in terms of this metaphysically represented identity.

The Sameness of thinking and Being that speaks in Parmenides' fragment stems from further back than the kind of identity defined by metaphysics in terms of Being as a characteristic of Being.

The key word in Parmenides' fragment, τὸ αὐτό, the Same, remains obscure. We shall leave it obscure. But we shall at the same time take a hint from the sentence that begins with this key word.

But meanwhile we have already fixed the Sameness of thinking and Being as the belonging together of the two. That was rash, perhaps of necessity. We must repair that rashness. And we can do so, since we do not consider the belonging together of which we have spoken as the ultimate or even the only authoritative interpretation of the Sameness of thinking and Being.

If we think of belonging *together* in the customary way, the meaning of belonging is determined by the word together, that is, by its unity. In that case, "to belong" means as much as: to be assigned and placed into the order of a "together," established in the unity of a manifold, combined into the unity of a system, mediated by the unifying center of an authoritative synthesis. Philosophy represents this belonging together as *nexus* and *connexio*, the necessary connection of the one with the other.

However, belonging together can also be thought of as *belonging* together. This means: the "together" is now determined by the belonging. Of course, we must still ask here what "belong" means in that case, and how its peculiar "together" is determined only in its terms. The answer to these questions is closer to us than we imagine, but it is not obvious. Enough for now that this reference makes us note the possibility of no longer representing belonging in terms of the unity of the together, but rather of experiencing this together in terms of belonging. However, does not the reference to this possibility amount to no more than an empty play on words, an artifice without support in verifiable facts?

That is how things look—until we take a closer look and let the matter speak for itself.

The idea of belonging together in the sense of a *belonging* together arises in respect of a situation which has already been mentioned. That situation is of course difficult to keep in mind, because it is so simple. But it comes closer to us just as soon as we pay heed to the following: In the interpretation of belonging together as *belonging* together we, taking Parmenides' hint, already had in mind thinking as well as Being, and thus what belongs to each other in the Same.

When we understand thinking to be the distinctive characteristic of man, we remind ourselves of a *belonging* together that concerns man and Being. Immediately we find ourselves grappling with the questions: What does Being mean? Who, or what, is man? Everybody can see easily that without a sufficient answer to these questions we lack the foundation for determining anything reliable about the *belonging* together of man and Being. But as long as we ask our questions in this way, we are confined within the attempt to represent the "together" of man and Being as a coordination, and to establish and explain this coordination either in terms of man or in terms of Being. In this procedure, the traditional concepts of man and Being constitute the toe-hold for the coordination of the two.

How would it be if, instead of tenaciously representing merely a coordination of the two in order to produce their unity, we were for once to note whether and how a belonging to one another first of all is at stake in this "together"? There is even the possibility that we might catch sight of the belonging together of man and Being, though only from afar, already in the traditional definitions of their essence. How so?

Man obviously is a being. As such he belongs to the totality of Being—just like the stone, the tree, or the eagle. To "belong" here still means to be in the order of Being. But man's distinctive feature lies in this, that he, as the being who thinks, is open to Being, face to face with Being; thus man remains referred to Being and so answers to it. Man *is* essentially this relationship of responding to Being, and he is only this. This "only" does not mean a limitation, but rather an excess. A belonging to Being prevails within man, a belonging which listens to Being because it is appropriated to Being. And Being? Let us think of Being according to its original meaning, as presence. Being is present to man neither incidentally nor only on rare occasions. Being is present and abides only as it concerns man through the claim it makes on him. For it is man, open toward Being, who alone lets Being arrive as presence. Such becoming present needs the openness of a clearing, and by this need remains appropriated to human being. This does not at all mean that Being is posited first and only by man. On the contrary, the following becomes clear:

Man and Being are appropriated to each other. They belong to each other. From this belonging to each other, which has not been thought out more closely, man and Being have first received those determinations of essence by which man and Being are grasped metaphysically in philosophy.

We stubbornly misunderstand this prevailing *belonging* together of man and Being as long as we represent everything only in categories and mediations, be it with or without dialectic. Then we always find only connections that are established either in terms of Being or in terms of man, and that present the belonging together of man and Being as an intertwining.

We do not as yet enter the domain of the *belonging* together. How can such an entry come about? By our moving away from the attitude of representational thinking. This move is a leap in the sense of a spring. The spring leaps away, away from the habitual idea of man as the rational animal who in modern times has become a subject for his objects. Simultaneously, the spring also leaps away from Being. But Being, since the beginning of Western thought, has been interpreted as the ground in which every being as such is grounded.

Where does the spring go that springs away from the ground? Into an abyss? Yes, as long as we only represent the spring in the horizon of metaphysical thinking. No, insofar as we spring and let go. Where to? To where we already have access: the belonging to

Being. Being itself, however, belongs to us; for only with us can Being be present as Being, that is, become present.

Thus a spring is needed in order to experience authentically the *belonging* together of man and Being. This spring is the abruptness of the unbridged entry into that belonging which alone can grant a toward-each-other of man and Being, and thus the constellation of the two. The spring is the abrupt entry into the realm from which man and Being have already reached each other in their active nature,[1] since both are mutually appropriated, extended as a gift, one to the other. Only the entry into the realm of this mutual appropriation determines and defines the experience of thinking.

What a curious leap, presumably yielding us the insight that we do not reside sufficiently as yet where in reality we already are. Where are we? In what constellation of Being and man?

Today we no longer need complicated directives, as we did some years ago, to catch sight of the constellation by virtue of which man and Being concern each other. Or so it seems. It is enough, one would think, to say the words "atomic age" in order to let us experience how Being becomes present to us today in the world of technology. But may we simply equate the world of technology with Being? Obviously not, not even if we imagine this world as the

---

[1] Heidegger's term is "Wesen." It is used in the verbal meaning of φύσις rather than the more static meaning of nature or essence. (Tr.)

totality in which atomic energy, the calculating plans of man, and automation are conjoined. Why does such a directive concerning the world of technology, even if it were the most circumstantial description, never let us catch sight of the constellation of Being and man? Because every analysis of the situation falls in its thinking short of the mark, in that the above-mentioned totality of the world of technology is interpreted in advance in terms of man, as being of man's making. Technology, conceived in the broadest sense and in its manifold manifestations, is taken for the plan which man projects, the plan which finally compels man to decide whether he will become the servant of his plan or will remain its master.

By this conception of the totality of the technological world, we reduce everything down to man, and at best come to the point of calling for an ethics of the technological world. Caught up in this conception, we confirm our own opinion that technology is of man's making alone. We fail to hear the claim of Being which speaks in the essence of technology.

Let us at long last stop conceiving technology as something purely technical, that is, in terms of man and his machines. Let us listen to the claim placed in our age not only upon man, but also upon all beings, nature and history, with regard to their Being.

What claim do we have in mind? Our whole human existence everywhere sees itself challenged—now playfully and now urgently, now breathlessly and now ponderously—to devote itself to the planning and calculating of everything. What speaks in this challenge? Does it stem merely from man's spontaneous whim? Or are we here already concerned with beings themselves, in such a way that they make a claim on us with respect to their aptness to be planned and calculated? Is it that Being itself is faced with the challenge of letting beings appear within the horizon of what is calculable? Indeed. And not only this. To the same degree that Being is challenged, man, too, is challenged, that is, forced to secure all beings that are his concern as the substance for his planning and calculating; and to carry this manipulation on past all bounds.

The name for the gathering of this challenge which places man and Being face to face in such a way that they challenge each other by turns is "the framework."

That in which and from which man and Being are of concern to each other in the technological world claims us in the manner of the framework. In the mutual confrontation of man and Being we discern the claim that determines the constellation of our age. The framework concerns us everywhere, immediately. The frame, if we may still speak in this manner, is more real than all of atomic energy and the whole world of machinery, more real than the driving power of organization, communications, and automation. Because we no longer encounter what is called the frame within the purview of representation which lets us think the Being of beings as presence—the frame no longer concerns us as something that is present—therefore the frame seems at first strange. It remains strange above all because it is not an ultimate, but rather first gives us That which prevails throughout the constellation of Being and man.

The *belonging* together of man and Being in the manner of mutual challenge drives home to us with startling force that and how man is delivered over to the ownership of Being and Being is appropriate to the essence of man. Within the framework there prevails a strange ownership and a strange appropriation. We must experience simply this owning in which man and Being are delivered over to each other, that is, we must enter into what we call *the event of appropriation*. The words event of appropriation, thought of in terms of the matter indicated, should now speak as a key term in the service of thinking. As such a key term, it can no more be translated than the Greek λόγος or the Chinese Tao. The term event of appropriation here no longer means what we would otherwise call a happening, an occurrence. It now is used as a *singulare tantum*. What it indicates happens only in the singular, no, not in any number, but uniquely. What we experience in the frame as the constellation of Being and man through the modern world of technology is a prelude to what is called the event of appropriation. This event, however, does not necessarily persist in its prelude. For in the event of appropriation the possibility arises that it may overcome the mere dominance of the frame to turn it into a more original appropriating. Such a transformation of the frame into the event of appropriation, by virtue of that event, would bring the appropriate recovery—appropriate, hence never to be produced by man alone—of the world of technology from its dominance back to servitude in the realm by which man reaches more truly into the event of appropriation.

Where are we now? At the entry of our thinking into that simplicity which we call in the strict sense of the term the event of appropriation. It seems as if we were now in danger of directing our thinking, all too carelessly, toward something that is remote and general; while in fact what the term event of appropriation wishes to indicate really speaks to us directly from the very nearness of that neighborhood in which we already reside. For what could be closer to us than what brings us nearer to where we belong, to where we are belongers, to the event of appropriation?

The event of appropriation is that realm, vibrating within itself, through which man and Being reach each other in their nature, achieve their active nature by losing those qualities with which metaphysics has endowed them.

To think of appropriating as the event of appropriation means to contribute to this self-vibrating realm. Thinking receives the tools for this self-suspended structure from language. For language is the most delicate and thus[1] the most susceptible vibration holding everything within the suspended structure of the appropriation. We dwell in the appropriation inasmuch as our active nature is given over to language.

We have now reached a point on our path where we must ask the crude but inevitable question: What does appropriation have to do with identity? Answer: Nothing. Identity, on the other hand, has much, perhaps everything, to do with appropriation. How so? We can answer this question by retracing our path in a few steps.

The appropriation appropriates man and Being to their essential togetherness. In the frame, we glimpse a first, oppressing flash of the appropriation. The frame constitutes the active nature of the modern world of technology. In the frame we witness a *belonging* together of man and Being in which the letting belong first determines the manner of the "together" and its unity. We let Parmenides' fragment "For the Same are thinking as well as Being" introduce us to the question of a belonging together in which belonging has precedence over "together." The question of the

---

[1] In conversation with the translator, Professor Heidegger here amended the published text of this essay, substituting the words *"und daher"* for the original *"aber auch."* The German text reprinted below retains the original published version. (Tr.)

meaning of this Same is the question of the active nature of identity. The doctrine of metaphysics represents identity as a fundamental characteristic of Being. Now it becomes clear that Being belongs with thinking to an identity whose active essence stems from that letting belong together which we call the appropriation. The essence of identity is a property of the event of appropriation.

If the attempt to guide our thinking to the abode of the essential origin of identity is to some extent tenable, what would have become of the title of our lecture? The meaning of the title "The principle of identity" would have undergone a transformation.

The law appears at first in the form of a fundamental principle which presupposes identity as a characteristic of Being, that is, of the ground of beings. This principle in the sense of a statement has in the meantime become a principle bearing the characteristics of a spring that departs from Being as the ground of beings, and thus springs into the abyss. But this abyss is neither empty nothingness nor murky confusion, but rather: the event of appropriation. In the event of appropriation vibrates the active nature of what speaks as language, which at one time was called the house of Being. "Principle of identity" means now: a spring demanded by the essence of identity because it needs that spring if the *belonging* together of man and Being is to attain the essential light of the appropriation.

On its way from the principle as a statement about identity to the principle as a spring into the essential origin of identity, thinking has undergone a transformation. Thus looking toward the present, beyond the situation of man, thinking sees the constellation of Being and man in terms of that which joins the two—by virtue of the event of appropriation.

Assuming we could look forward to the possibility that the frame—the mutual challenge of man and Being to enter the calculation of what is calculable—were to address itself to us as the event of appropriation which first surrenders man and Being to their own being; then a path would be open for man to experience beings in a more originary way—the totality of the modern technological world, nature and history, and above all their Being.

As long as reflection on the world of the atomic age, however earnestly and responsibly, strives for no more than the peaceful use of atomic energy, and also will not be content with any other goal, thinking stops halfway. Such halfwayness only secures the technological world all the more in its metaphysical predominance.

But what authority has decided that nature as such must forever *remain* the nature of modern physics, and that history must forever appear only as subject matter for historians? We cannot, of course, reject today's technological world as devil's work, nor may we destroy it—assuming it does not destroy itself.

Still less may we cling to the view that the world of technology is such that it will absolutely prevent a spring out of it. For this view is obsessed by the latest news, and regards them as the only thing that is real. This view is indeed fantastical; but the same is not true of a thinking ahead, looking toward that which approaches us as the call of the active nature of identity between man and Being.

Thinking has needed more than two thousand years really to understand such a simple relation as that of the mediation within identity. Do *we* then have a right to the opinion that the thinking entry into the essential source of identity could be achieved in a day? Precisely because this entry requires a spring, it must take its time, the time of thinking which is different from the time of calculation that pulls our thinking in all directions. Today, the computer calculates thousands of relationships in one second. Despite their technical uses, they are inessential.

Whatever and however we may try to think, we think within the sphere of tradition. Tradition prevails when it frees us from thinking back to a thinking forward, which is no longer a planning.

Only when we turn thoughtfully toward what has already been thought, will we be turned to use for what must still be thought.

THE ONTO-THEO-LOGICAL
CONSTITUTION OF METAPHYSICS

This seminar made an attempt to begin a conversation with *Hegel.* A conversation with a thinker can be concerned only with the matter of thinking. The matter of thinking presses upon thinking in such a way that only thus does it bring thinking to the heart of the matter and from there to thinking itself.

For Hegel, the matter of thinking is: Thinking as such. In order not to misinterpret this definition of the matter—thinking as such —in psychological or epistemological terms, we must add by way of explanation: thinking as such—in the developed fullness in which what has been thought, has been and now is thought. What this means here we can understand only from Kant's viewpoint, from the essence of the transcendental which Hegel, however, thinks absolutely, and that for him means speculatively. This is Hegel's aim when he says of the thinking of thinking as such that it is developed "purely in the element of thinking." (*Encyclopedia,* Introduction, 14.) To give it a short title, which yet is very difficult to think through rigorously, this means: the matter of thinking is for Hegel "the idea" (*der Gedanke*). "The idea," developed to its highest essential freedom, becomes "the absolute Idea" (*Idee*). Near the end of the *Science of Logic* (Lasson edition, Vol. II, 484), Hegel says of the absolute Idea: "Only the absolute Idea is *Being*, imperishable *Life, self-knowing Truth*, and it is *all Truth*." Thus Hegel himself explicitly gives to the matter of his thinking that name which is inscribed over the whole matter of Western thinking, the name: *Being*.

(In our seminar, the manifold yet unified use of the word "Being" was discussed. For Hegel, Being means first, but *never exclusively*, "indeterminate immediacy." Being is seen here from the viewpoint of determining mediation, that is, from the viewpoint of the absolute concept, and thus with reference to the absolute concept. "The truth of Being is essence," that is, absolute reflection. The truth of essence is the concept in the sense of in-finite self-knowledge. Being is the absolute self-thinking of thinking. Absolute thinking alone is the truth of Being, "is" Being. Truth here means always that the knowable as such is known with a knowledge absolutely certain of itself.)

At the same time, Hegel rigorously thinks about the matter of his thinking in the context of a conversation with the previous history of thinking. Hegel is the first thinker who can and must think in this way. Hegel's relation to the history of philosophy is the speculative, and only as such a historical, relation. The character of the movement of history is an occurrence in the sense of the dialectical process. Hegel writes: "The same development of thinking which is portrayed in the history of philosophy is portrayed in philosophy itself, but freed from that element of historical externality, *purely in the element of thinking.*" (*Encyclopedia*, 14.)

We stop, baffled. According to Hegel's own words, philosophy itself and the history of philosophy are supposed to be related to each other externally. But the externality of which Hegel thinks is by no means external in the crude sense of being something merely superficial and indifferent. Externality here means that outside dimension in which all history and every real course of events have their place in comparison to the movement of the absolute Idea. The externality of history as explained here, in relation to the Idea, emerges as the result of the Idea's self-externalization. Externality is itself a dialectical determination. We thus fall far short of Hegel's real thought if we state that Hegel has brought historical representation and systematic thinking into a unity in philosophy. For Hegel is concerned neither with historiography, nor with the system in the sense of a doctrinal structure.

What is the purpose of these remarks about philosophy and its relation to history? They mean to suggest that, for Hegel, the matter of thinking is in itself historical—but historical in the sense of occurrence. The process-character of thinking is determined by the dialectic of Being. For Hegel, the matter of thinking is: Being, as thinking thinking itself; and thinking comes to itself only in the process of its speculative development, thus running through stages of the variously developed, and hence of necessity previously undeveloped, forms.

Only from the matter of thinking thus experienced does a peculiar principle arise for Hegel—the criterion for the manner in which he speaks with those thinkers that preceded him.

Therefore, when we attempt a thinking conversation with Hegel, we must speak with him not just about the same matter, but about the same matter in the same way. But the same is not the merely identical. In the merely identical, the difference disappears. In the same the difference appears, and appears all the more pressingly, the more resolutely thinking is concerned with the same matter in the same way. Hegel thinks of the Being of beings speculative-historically. But inasmuch as Hegel's thinking belongs to a period of history (this does not mean at all that it belongs to the past), we are attempting to think of Being, as Hegel thought of it, in the same manner, that is, to think of it historically.

Thinking can stay with its matter only if it becomes ever more rigorous in its constancy, only if the same matter becomes for it ever more sharply contested. In this way the matter requires thinking to stay with it in its own manner of being, to remain steadfast toward that manner of being, answering to it by sustaining the matter to its completion. If its matter is Being, the thinking which stays with its matter must involve itself in the perdurance of Being. Accordingly, in a conversation with Hegel we are expected to clarify in advance the sameness of the same matter for the sake of that conversation. According to what has been said, we are required in our conversation with the history of philosophy to elucidate the otherness of the historical at the same time as we elucidate the otherness of the matter of thinking. Such a clarification must of necessity turn out to be short and sketchy.

In order to clarify the diversity that prevails betweeen Hegel's thinking and our own attempt at thinking, we shall note three things.

We shall ask,

1. What is the matter of thinking for Hegel, and what is it for us?

2. What is the criterion for the conversation with the history of thinking for Hegel, and what is it for us?

3. What is the character of this conversation for Hegel, and what is it for us?

To the first question:

For Hegel, the matter of thinking is: Being with respect to beings having been thought in absolute thinking, and as absolute thinking. For us, the matter of thinking is the Same, and thus is Being—but Being with respect to its difference from beings. Put more precisely: for Hegel, the matter of thinking is the idea as the absolute concept. For us, formulated in a preliminary fashion, the matter of thinking is the difference *as* difference.

To the second question:

For Hegel, the criterion for the conversation with the history of philosophy is: to enter into the force and sphere of what has been thought by earlier thinkers. It is not by chance that Hegel advances his principle in the context of a conversation with Spinoza and before a conversation with Kant. (*Science of Logic*, book III, Lasson edition, vol. II, p. 216 ff.) In Spinoza, Hegel finds the fully developed "standpoint of substance" which cannot, however, be the highest standpoint because Being is not yet thought equally fundamentally and resolutely as thinking thinking itself. Being, as substance and substantiality, has not yet developed into the subject in its absolute subjectivity. Still, Spinoza appeals always afresh to the whole thinking of German Idealism, and at the same time provokes its contradiction, because he lets thinking begin with the absolute. Kant's path, in contrast, is different, and is even more decisive than Spinoza's system for the thinking of absolute idealism and for philosophy generally. Hegel sees in Kant's idea of the original synthesis of apperception "one of the most profound principles for speculative development." (*Ibid.*) For Hegel, the force of each thinker lies in what each has thought, in that their thought can be incorporated into absolute thinking as one of its stages. Absolute thinking is absolute only by moving within its dialectical-speculative process, and thus requiring stages.

For us, the criterion for the conversation with historical tradition is the same, insofar as it is a question of entering into the force of earlier thinking. We, however, do not seek that force in what has already been thought: we seek it in something that has not been thought, and from which what has been thought receives its essential space. But only what has already been thought prepares what has not yet been thought, which enters ever anew into its abundance. The criterion of what has not been thought does not lead to the inclusion of previous thought into a still higher development and systematization that surpass it. Rather, the criterion demands that traditional thinking be set free into its essential past which is still preserved. This essential past prevails throughout the tradition in an originary way, is always in being in advance of it, and yet is never expressly thought in its own right and as the Originary.

To the third question:

For Hegel, the conversation with the earlier history of philosophy has the character of *Aufhebung*,[1] that is, of the mediating concept in the sense of an absolute foundation.

For us, the character of the conversation with the history of thinking is no longer *Aufhebung* (elevation), but the step back.

Elevation leads to the heightening and gathering area of truth posited as absolute, truth in the sense of the completely developed certainty of self-knowing knowledge.

The step back points to the realm which until now has been skipped over, and from which the essence of truth becomes first of all worthy of thought.

After this brief characterization of the difference between Hegel's thinking and ours with respect to the matter, and with respect to the criterion and character, of a conversation with the history of thinking, let us now try to proceed with the conversation begun with Hegel and clarify it a little more. This means: we venture an

[1] Aufhebung. This *terminus technicus* of Hegel's philosophy has the triple meaning of negating something in its mere individuality as a partial reality (*negare*), of preserving it in its essential being (*conservare*), and of elevating it into the higher sphere of the whole of reality (*elevare*). (Tr.)

attempt with the step back. The term "step back" suggests various misinterpretations. "Step back" does not mean an isolated step of thought, but rather means the manner in which thinking moves, and a long path. Since the step back determines the character of our conversation with the history of Western thinking, our thinking in a way leads us away from what has been thought so far in philosophy. Thinking recedes before its matter, Being, and thus brings what is thought into a confrontation in which we behold the whole of this history—behold it with respect to what constitutes the source of this entire thinking, because it alone establishes and prepares for this thinking the area of its abode. In contrast to Hegel, this is not a traditional problem, already posed, but what has always remained unasked throughout this history of thinking. We speak of it, tentatively and unavoidably, in the language of tradition. We speak of the *difference* between Being and beings. The step back goes from what is unthought, from the difference as such, into what gives us thought.[2] That is the *oblivion* of the difference. The oblivion here to be thought is the veiling of the difference as such, thought in terms of Λήϑη (concealment); this veiling has in turn withdrawn itself from the beginning. The oblivion belongs to the difference because the difference belongs to the oblivion.

[2] *Das zu-Denkende* is that which gives thinking to us and it is that which is to be thought. (Tr.)

The oblivion does not happen to the difference only afterward, in consequence of the forgetfulness of human thinking.

The difference between beings and Being is the area within which metaphysics, Western thinking in its entire nature, can be what it is. The step back thus moves out of metaphysics into the essential nature of metaphysics. The remark about Hegel's use of the ambiguous key word "Being" shows that discourse about Being and beings can never be pinned down to *one* epoch in the history of the clearing of "Being." Nor does discourse about "Being" ever understand this name in the sense of a genus, an empty generality under which the historically represented doctrines of beings are subsumed as individual cases. "Being" ever and always speaks as destiny, and thus permeated by tradition.

But the step back out of metaphysics into its essential nature requires a duration and an endurance whose dimensions we do not know. Only one thing is clear: the step back calls for a preparation which must be ventured here and now; but it must be ventured in the face of beings as such and as a whole, as they *are* now and are visibly beginning to show themselves ever more unequivocally. What now *is*, is marked by the dominance of the active nature of modern technology. This dominance is already presenting itself in all areas of life, by various identifiable traits such as functionalization, systematic improvement, automation, bureaucratization,

51

communications. Just as we call the idea of living things biology, just so the presentation and full articulation of all beings, dominated as they now are everywhere by the nature of the technical, may be called technology. The expression may serve as a term for the metaphysics of the atomic age. Viewed from the present and drawn from our insight into the present, the step back out of metaphysics into the essential nature of metaphysics is the step out of technology and technological description and interpretation of the age, into the *essence* of modern technology which is still to be thought.

This remark ought to prevent the other obvious misinterpretation of the term "step back": the view that the step back consists in a historical return to the earliest thinkers of Western philosophy. The "whither" to which the step back directs us, develops and shows itself only in the execution of the step.

In order to gain perspective in the seminar on the whole of Hegelian metaphysics, we chose as a temporary expedient an interpretation of the section which opens the first book of the *Science of Logic*, "The doctrine of Being." The section title alone gives us in each of its words enough to think about. It reads: *"With what must the beginning of science be made?"* Hegel's answer to this question consists in the demonstration that the beginning is "of a speculative nature." This means: the beginning is neither something immediate nor something mediated. We tried to express this nature of the beginning in a speculative sentence: "The beginning is the result." In accordance with the dialectical plurality of meanings of the "is," this means several things. It means for one thing: the beginning—taking *resultare* in its literal meaning[1]—is the rebound of thinking thinking itself out of the completion of the dialectical movement. The completion of this movement, the absolute Idea, is the totality developed within itself, the fullness of Being. The rebound from this fullness results in the emptiness of Being. In science (the absolute, self-knowing knowledge) the beginning must be made with this emptiness. The beginning and the end of the movement, and before them the movement itself, always remains Being. It has its being as the movement, revolving within itself, from fullness into the most extreme self-externalization and again from there into self-completing fullness. The matter of thinking thus is for Hegel thinking thinking itself as Being revolving within itself. In an inversion which is not only legitimate but necessary, the speculative sentence concerning the beginning runs: "The result is the beginning." The beginning must really be made with the result, since the beginning results from that result.

This says the same as the remark which Hegel adds in an aside and in parentheses, near the end of the section about the beginning: "(and *God* would have the uncontested right to have the beginning

<hr/>

[1] *resultare*—to leap back, to rebound.

made with him)" (Lasson edition, vol. I, 63). According to the question that is the title of the section, we are now dealing with the "beginning of science." If science must begin with God, then it is the science of God: theology. This name is taken here in its later meaning of theo-logy as statements of representational thinking about God. Θεόλογος, Θεολογία mean at this point the mytho-poetic utterance about the gods, with no reference to any creed or ecclesiastical doctrine.

Why is "science"—which since Fichte is the name for meta-physics—why is science theology? Answer: because science is the systematic development of knowledge, the Being of beings knows itself as this knowledge, and thus it is in truth. The schoolmen's name which during the transition from the medieval to the modern period emerges for the science of Being, that is, for the science of beings as such in general, is ontosophy or ontology. Western meta-physics, however, since its beginning with the Greeks has eminently been both ontology and theology, still without being tied to these rubrics. For this reason my inaugural lecture *What is Metaphysics?* (1929) defines metaphysics as the question about beings as such *and* as a whole. The wholeness of this whole is the unity of all beings that unifies as the generative ground. To those who can read, this means: metaphysics is onto-theo-logy. Someone who has experienced theology in his own roots, both the theology of the

Christian faith and that of philosophy, would today rather remain silent about God when he is speaking in the realm of thinking. For the onto-theological character of metaphysics has become questionable for thinking, not because of any kind of atheism, but from the experience of a thinking which has discerned in onto-theo-logy the still *unthought* unity of the essential nature of metaphysics. This nature of metaphysics, however, still remains what is most worthy of thought for thinking, as long as thinking does not break off the conversation with its tradition, permeated by destiny, in an arbitrary manner thus unrelated to destiny.

In the fifth (1949) edition of *What is Metaphysics?*, a new introduction explicitly refers to the onto-theological nature of metaphysics. But it would be rash to assert that metaphysics is theology because it is ontology. One would say first: Metaphysics is theology, a statement about God, because the deity enters into philosophy. Thus the question about the onto-theological character of metaphysics is sharpened to the question: How does the deity enter into philosophy, not just modern philosophy, but philosophy as such? This question can be answered only after it has first been sufficiently developed as a question.

We can properly think through the question, How does the deity enter into philosophy?, only when that *to which* the deity is to come has become sufficiently clear: that is, philosophy itself. As long as we search through the history of philosophy merely historically, we shall find everywhere that the deity has entered into it. But assuming that philosophy, as thinking, is the free and spontaneous self-involvement with beings as such, then the deity can come into philosophy only insofar as philosophy, of its own accord and by its own nature, requires and determines that and how the deity enters into it. The question, How does the deity enter into philosophy?, leads back to the question, What is the origin of the onto-theological essential constitution of metaphysics? To accept this kind of question means to accomplish the step back.

In this step, we turn our thought to the essential origin of the onto-theological structure of all metaphysics. We ask: How does the deity, and therewith accordingly theology, and with theology the onto-theological character, enter into metaphysics? We raise this question in the context of a conversation with the whole of the history of philosophy. But we are questioning at the same time with a particular regard to Hegel. Here we are prompted to give thought first to a curious fact.

Hegel thinks of Being in its most empty emptiness, that is, in its most general aspect. At the same time, he thinks of Being in its fully completed fullness. Still, he does not call speculative philosophy, that is, philosophy proper, onto-theo-logy but rather "Science of Logic." By giving it this name, Hegel brings to light something decisive. It would be easy, of course, to explain the designation of metaphysics as "logic" by pointing out that for Hegel the matter of thinking is "the idea," understanding that word as a *singulare tantum*. The idea, thinking, is obviously and by ancient custom the theme of logic. Certainly. But it is just as incontestable that Hegel, faithful to tradition, sees the matter of thinking in beings as such and as a whole, in the movement of Being from its emptiness to its developed fullness.

But how can "Being" ever come to present itself as "thought"? How else than by the fact that Being is previously marked as ground, while thinking—since it belongs together with Being— gathers itself toward Being as its ground, in the manner of giving ground and accounting for the ground.[3] Being manifests itself as thought. This means: the Being of beings reveals itself as the ground that gives itself ground and accounts for itself. The ground, the *ratio* by their essential origin are the Λόγος, in the sense of the gathering of beings and letting them be. They are the Ἐν Πάντα. Thus "science," that is, metaphysics, is in truth "logic"

---

[3] There are three closely related terms in the German text: *"begründen"* (to account for), *"ergründen"* (to give the ground), and *"gründen"* (to ground). In a consultation Heidegger clarified the relation of these terms as follows: *"Begründen"* has to do with beings and is ontic. *"Ergründen"* belongs to Being and is ontological. *"Gründen"* is the relationship of *"begründen"* and *"ergründen"* and encompasses both. (Tr.)

for Hegel not because the theme of science is thinking, but because *Being* remains the matter of thinking; while Being, ever since the early days when it became unconcealed in the character of Λόγος, the ground that grounds, claims thinking—the accounting of the ground—for itself.

Metaphysics thinks of beings as such, that is, in general. Metaphysics thinks of beings as such, as a whole. Metaphysics thinks of the Being of beings both in the ground-giving unity of what is most general, what is indifferently valid everywhere, and also in the unity of the all that accounts for the ground, that is, of the All-Highest. The Being of beings is thus thought of in advance as the grounding ground. Therefore all metaphysics is at bottom, and from the ground up, what grounds, what gives account of the ground, what is called to account by the ground, and finally what calls the ground to account.

Why do we mention this? So that we may experience the shopworn terms ontology, theology, onto-theology in their true gravity. At first and commonly, the terms ontology and theology do, of course, look like other familiar terms: psychology, biology, cosmology, archeology. The last syllable, -logy, means broadly and usually that we are dealing with the science of the soul, of living things, of the cosmos, of ancient things. But -logy hides more than just the logical in the sense of what is consistent and generally in the nature of a statement, what structures, moves, secures, and communicates all scientific knowledge. In each case, the -Logia is the totality of a nexus of grounds accounted for, within which nexus the objects of the sciences are represented in respect of their ground, that is, are conceived. Ontology, however, and theology are "Logies" inasmuch as they provide the ground of beings as such and account for them within the whole. They account for Being as the ground of beings. They account to the Λόγος, and are in an essential sense in accord with the Λόγος-, that is they are the logic of the Λόγος. Thus they are more precisely called onto-logic and theo-logic. More rigorously and clearly thought out, metaphysics is: onto-theo-logic.

We now understand the name "logic" in the essential sense which includes also the title used by Hegel, and only thus explains it: as the name for that kind of thinking which everywhere provides and accounts for the ground of beings as such within the whole in terms of Being as the ground (Λόγος). The fundamental character of metaphysics is onto-theo-logic. We should now be in a position to explain how the deity enters into philosophy.

To what extent is an explanation successful? To the extent that we take heed of the following: the matter of thinking is beings as such, that is, Being. Being shows itself in the nature of the ground. Accordingly, the matter of thinking, Being as the ground, is thought out fully only when the ground is represented as the first ground, πρώτη ἀρχή. The original matter of thinking presents itself as the first cause, the *causa prima* that corresponds to the reason-giving path back to the *ultima ratio*, the final accounting. The Being of beings is represented fundamentally, in the sense of the ground, only as *causa sui*. This is the metaphysical concept of God. Metaphysics must think in the direction of the deity because the matter of thinking is Being; but Being is in being as ground in diverse ways: as Λόγος, as ὑποκείμενον, as substance, as subject.

This explanation, though it supposedly touches upon something that is correct, is quite inadequate for the interpretation of the essential nature of metaphysics, because metaphysics is not only theo-logic but also onto-logic. Metaphysics, first of all, is neither only the one nor the other *also*. Rather, metaphysics is theo-logic because it is onto-logic. It is onto-logic because it is theo-logic. The onto-theological essential constitution of metaphysics cannot be explained in terms of either theologic or ontologic, even if an explanation could ever do justice here to what remains to be thought out.

For it still remains unthought by what unity ontologic and theo-logic belong together, what the origin of this unity is, and what the difference of the differentiated which this unity unifies. All of this still remains unthought. The problem here is obviously not a union of two independent disciplines of metaphysics, but the unity of *what* is in question, and in thought, in ontologic and theologic: beings as such in the universal and primal *at one with* beings as such in the highest and ultimate. The unity of this One is of such a kind that the ultimate in its own way accounts for the primal, and the primal in its own way accounts for the ultimate. The difference between the two ways of accounting belongs to the still-unthought difference we mentioned.

The essential constitution of metaphysics is based on the unity of beings as such in the universal and that which is highest.

Our task here is to deal with the question about the onto-theological nature of metaphysics first of all simply as a question. Only the matter itself can direct us to the point with which the question about the onto-theological constitution of metaphysics deals. It can do so in this way, that we attempt to think of the matter of thinking in a more rigorous manner. The matter of thinking has been handed down to Western thinking under the name "Being." If we think of this matter just a bit more rigorously, if we take more heed of what is in contest in the matter, we see that *Being* means always and everywhere: the Being of *beings*. The genitive in this phrase is to be taken as a *genitivus objectivus*. *Beings* means always and everywhere the beings *of Being*; here the genitive is to be taken as a *genitivus subjectivus*. It is, however, with certain reservations that we speak of a genitive in respect to object and subject, because these terms, subject and object, in their turn stem from a particular character of Being. Only this much is clear, that when we deal with the Being of beings and with the beings of Being, we deal in each case with a difference.

Thus we think of Being rigorously only when we think of it in its difference with beings, and of beings in their difference with Being. The difference thus comes specifically into view. If we try to form a representational idea of it, we will at once be misled into conceiving of difference as a relation which our representing has added to Being and to beings. Thus the difference is reduced to a distinction, something made up by our understanding (*Verstand*).

But if we assume that the difference is a contribution made by our representational thinking, the question arises: a contribution to what? One answers: to beings. Good. But what does that mean: "beings"? What else could it mean than: something that *is*? Thus we give to the supposed contribution, the representational idea of difference, a place within Being. But "Being" itself says: Being which is *beings*. Whenever we come to the place to which we were supposedly first bringing difference along as an alleged contribution, we always find that Being and beings in their difference are already there. It is as in Grimm's fairytale *The Hedgehog and the Hare*: "I'm here already." Now it would be possible to deal with this strange state of affairs—that Being and beings are always found to be already there by virtue of and within the difference— in a crude manner and explain it as follows: our representational thinking just happens to be so structured and constituted that it will always, so to speak over its own head and out of its own head, insert the difference ahead of time between beings and Being. Much might be said, and much more might be asked, about this seemingly convincing but also rashly given explanation—and first of all, we might ask: where does the "between" come from, into which the difference is, so to speak, to be inserted?

We shall discard all views and explanations, and instead note the following: this thing that is called difference, we encounter it everywhere and always in the matter of thinking, in beings as such —encounter it so unquestioningly that we do not even notice this encounter itself. Nor does anything compel us to notice it. Our thinking is free either to pass over the difference without a thought or to think of it specifically as such. But this freedom does not apply in every case. Unexpectedly it may happen that thinking finds itself called upon to ask: what does it say, this Being that is mentioned so often? If Being here shows itself concurrently as the Being of . . . , thus in the genitive of the difference, then the preceding question is more properly: what do you make of the difference if Being as well as beings appear *by virtue of the difference,* each in its own way? To do justice to this question, we must first assume a proper position face to face with the difference. Such a confrontation becomes manifest to us once we accomplish the step back. Only as this step gains for us greater distance does what is near give itself as such, does nearness achieve its first radiance. By the step back, we set the matter of thinking, Being as difference, free to enter a position face to face, which may well remain wholly without an object.

While we are facing the difference, though by the step back we are already releasing it into that which gives thought, we can say: the Being of beings means Being which is beings. The "is" here speaks transitively, in transition. Being here becomes present in the manner of a transition to beings. But Being does not leave its own place and go over to beings, as though beings were first without Being and could be approached by Being subsequently. Being transits (that), comes unconcealingly over (that) which arrives as something of itself unconcealed only by that coming-over.[4] Arrival means: to keep concealed in unconcealedness—to abide present in this keeping—to be a being.

Being shows itself as the unconcealing overwhelming. Beings as

---

[4] *Überkommnis,* coming-over, overwhelming (Tr.)

such appear in the manner of the arrival that keeps itself concealed in unconcealedness.

Being in the sense of unconcealing overwhelming, and beings as such in the sense of arrival that keeps itself concealed, are present, and thus differentiated, by virtue of the Same, the differentiation. That differentiation alone grants and holds apart the "between," in which the overwhelming and the arrival are held toward one another, are borne away from and toward each other. The difference of Being and beings, as the differentiation of overwhelming and arrival, is the perdurance (Austrag) of the two in *unconcealing keeping in concealment.* Within this perdurance there prevails a clearing of what veils and closes itself off—and this its prevalence bestows the being apart, and the being toward each other, of overwhelming and arrival.

In our attempt to think of the difference as such, we do not make it disappear; rather, we follow it to its essential origin. On our way there we think of the perdurance of overwhelming and arrival. This is the matter of thinking, thought closer to rigorous thinking —closer by the distance of one step back: Being thought in terms of the difference.

We here need to insert a remark, however, concerning what we said about the matter of thinking—a remark that again and again calls for our attention. When we say "Being," we use the word in

65

its widest and least definite general meaning. But even when we speak merely of a general meaning, we have thought of Being in an inappropriate way. We represent Being in a way in which It, Being, never gives itself. The manner in which the matter of thinking—Being—comports itself, remains a unique state of affairs. Initially, our customary ways of thinking are never able to clarify it more than inadequately. This we shall try to show by an example, bearing in mind from the start that nowhere in beings is there an example for the active nature of Being, because the nature of Being is itself the unprecedented exemplar.

Hegel at one point mentions the following case to characterize the generality of what is general: Someone wants to buy fruit in a store. He asks for fruit. He is offered apples and pears, he is offered peaches, cherries, grapes. But he rejects all that is offered. He absolutely wants to have fruit. What was offered to him in every instance *is* fruit and yet, it turns out, fruit cannot be bought.

It is still infinitely more impossible to represent "Being" as the general characteristic of particular beings. There is Being only in this or that particular historic character: Φύσις, Λόγος, Ἐν, Ἰδέα, Ἐνέργεια, Substantiality, Objectivity, Subjectivity, the Will, the Will to Power, the Will to Will. But these historic forms cannot be found in rows, like apples, pears, peaches, lined up on the counter of historical representational thinking.

And yet, did we not hear of Being in the historical order and sequence of the dialectical process that is in Hegel's thought? Certainly. But here, too, Being gives itself only in the light that cleared itself for Hegel's thinking. That is to say: the manner in which it, Being, gives itself, is itself determined by the way in which it clears itself. This way, however, is a historic, always epochal character which has being for us as such only when we release it into its own native past. We attain to the nearness of the historic only in that sudden moment of a recall in thinking. The same also holds true for the experience of the given character of that difference of Being and beings to which corresponds a given interpretation of beings as such. What has been said holds true above all also for our attempt in the step back out of the oblivion of the difference as such, to think this difference as the perdurance of unconcealing overcoming and of self-keeping arrival. If we listen more closely, we shall realize, of course, that in this discussion about perdurance we have already allowed the essential past to speak inasmuch as we are thinking of unconcealing and keeping concealed, of transition (transcendence), and of arrival (presence). In fact, it may be that this discussion, which assigns the difference of Being and beings to perdurance as the approach to their essence, even brings to light something all-pervading which pervades Being's destiny from its beginning to its completion. Yet it remains difficult to say how this all-pervasiveness is to be thought, if it is neither something universal, valid in all cases, nor a law guaranteeing the necessity of a process in the sense of the dialectical.

The only thing that now matters for our task is an insight into a possibility of thinking of the difference as a perdurance so as to clarify to what extent the onto-theological constitution of metaphysics has its essential origin in the perdurance that begins the history of metaphysics, governs all of its epochs, and yet remains everywhere concealed *as* perdurance, and thus forgotten in an oblivion which even escapes itself.

In order to facilitate that insight, let us think of Being, and in Being of the difference, and in the difference of perdurance in terms of that character of Being through which Being has cleared itself as Λόγος, as the ground. Being shows itself in the un-concealing overwhelming as that which allows whatever arrives to lie before us, as the grounding in the manifold ways in which beings are brought about before us. Beings as such, the arrival that keeps itself concealed in unconcealedness, is what is grounded; so grounded and so generated, it in turn grounds in its own way, that is, it effects, it causes. The perdurance of that which grounds and that which is grounded, as such, not only holds the two apart, it holds them facing each other. What is held apart is held in the tension of perdurance in such a way that not only does Being

68

ground beings as their ground, but beings in their turn ground, cause Being in their way. Beings can do so only insofar as they "are" the fullness of Being: they are what *is* most of all.

Here our reflections reach an exciting juncture. Being becomes present as Λόγος in the sense of ground, of allowing to let lie before us. The same Λόγος, as the gathering of what unifies, is the ʽΕν. This ʽΕν, however, is twofold. For one thing, it is the unifying One in the sense of what is everywhere primal and thus most universal; and at the same time it is the unifying One in the sense of the All-Highest (Zeus). The Λόγος grounds and gathers everything into the universal, and accounts for and gathers everything in terms of the unique. It may be noted in passing that the same Λόγος also contains within itself the essential origin of the character of all language, and thus determines the way of utterance as a logical way in the broader sense.

Inasmuch as Being becomes present as the Being of beings, as the difference, as perduration, the separateness and mutual relatedness of grounding and of accounting for endures, Being grounds beings, and beings, as what *is* most of all, account for Being. One comes over the other, one arrives in the other. Overwhelming and arrival appear in each other in reciprocal reflection. Speaking in terms of the difference, this means: perdurance is a circling, the circling of Being and beings around each other. Grounding itself appears within the clearing of perdurance as something that *is*, thus itself as a being that requires the corresponding accounting for through a being, that is, causation, and indeed causation by the highest cause.

One of the classic examples in the history of metaphysics of this situation is found in a generally neglected text of Leibniz, which we shall call for short "The 24 Theses of Metaphysics" (Gerh. Phil. VII, 289 ff.; cf. M. Heidegger, *Der Satz vom Grund*, 1957, 51 ff.).

Metaphysics responds to Being as Λόγος, and is accordingly in its basic characteristics everywhere logic, but a logic that thinks of the Being of beings, and thus the logic which is determined by what differs in the difference: onto-theo-logic.

Since metaphysics thinks of beings as such as a whole, it represents beings in respect of what differs in the difference, and without heeding the difference as difference.

What differs shows itself as the Being of beings in general, and as the Being of beings in the Highest.

Because Being appears as ground, beings are what is grounded; the highest being, however, is what accounts in the sense of giving the first cause. When metaphysics thinks of beings with respect to the ground that is common to all beings as such, then it is logic as onto-logic. When metaphysics thinks of beings as such as a whole, that is, with respect to the highest being which accounts for everything, then it is logic as theo-logic.

Because the thinking of metaphysics remains involved in the difference which as such is unthought, metaphysics is both ontology and theology in a unified way, by virtue of the unifying unity of perdurance.

The onto-theological constitution of metaphysics stems from the prevalence of that difference which keeps Being as the ground, and beings as what is grounded and what gives account, apart from and related to each other; and by this keeping, perdurance is achieved.

That which bears such a name directs our thinking to the realm which the key words of metaphysics—Being and beings, the ground and what is grounded—are no longer adequate to utter. For what these words name, what the manner of thinking that is guided by them represents, originates as that which differs by virtue of the difference. The origin of the difference can no longer be thought of within the scope of metaphysics.

The insight into the onto-theological constitution of metaphysics shows a possible way to answer the question, "How does the deity enter into philosophy?," in terms of the essence of metaphysics.

The deity enters into philosophy through the perdurance of which we think at first as the approach to the active nature of the difference between Being and beings. The difference constitutes the ground plan in the structure of the essence of metaphysics. The perdurance results in and gives Being as the generative ground. This ground itself needs to be properly accounted for by that for which it accounts, that is, by the causation through the supremely original matter—and that is the cause as *causa sui*. This is the right name for the god of philosophy. Man can neither pray nor sacrifice to this god. Before the *causa sui*, man can neither fall to his knees in awe nor can he play music and dance before this god.

The god-less thinking which must abandon the god of philosophy, god as *causa sui*, is thus perhaps closer to the divine God. Here this means only: god-less thinking is more open to Him than onto-theo-logic would like to admit.

This remark may throw a little light on the path to which thinking is on its way, that thinking which accomplishes the step back, back out of metaphysics into the active essence of metaphysics, back out of the oblivion of the difference as such into the destiny of the withdrawing concealment of perdurance.

No one can know whether and when and where and how this step of thinking will develop into a proper (needed in appropriation) path and way and road-building. Instead, the rule of metaphysics may rather entrench itself, in the shape of modern technology with its developments rushing along boundlessly. Or, everything that results by way of the step back may merely be exploited and absorbed by metaphysics in its own way, as the result of representational thinking.

Thus the step back would itself remain unaccomplished, and the path which it opens and points out would remain untrod.

Such reflections impose themselves easily, but they carry no weight compared with an entirely different difficulty through which the step back must pass.

That difficulty lies in language. Our Western languages are languages of metaphysical thinking, each in its own way. It must remain an open question whether the nature of Western languages is in itself marked with the exclusive brand of metaphysics, and thus marked permanently by onto-theo-logic, or whether these languages offer other possibilities of utterance—and that means at the same time of a telling silence. The difficulty to which thoughtful utterance is subject has appeared often enough in the course of this seminar. The little word "is," which speaks everywhere in our language, and tells of Being even where It does not appear expressly, contains the whole destiny of Being—from the ἔστιν γάρ εἶναι of Parmenides to the "is" of Hegel's speculative sentence, and to the dissolution of the "is" in the positing of the Will to Power with Nietzsche.

Our facing this difficulty that stems from language should keep us from hastily recasting the language of the thinking here attempted into the coin of a terminology, and from speaking right away about perdurance, instead of devoting all our efforts to thinking through what has been said. For what was said, was said in a seminar. A seminar, as the word implies, is a place and an opportunity to sow a seed here and there, a seed of thinking which some time or other may bloom in its own way and bring forth fruit.

Concerning the attempt to think the thing, cf. *Das Ding*, to be published by Harper & Row. The lecture "The Thing" was first given in the context of a series of lectures entitled "Insight into that which is" in Bremen in December, 1949, and in Bühlerhöhe, Spring, 1950.

Concerning the interpretation of Parmenides, cf. *Moira*.

Concerning the essence of modern technology and modern science, cf. *Die Frage nach der Technik*.

Concerning the determination of Being as ground, cf. *Logos* and *Der Satz vom Grund*.

Concerning the explanation of the difference, cf. *What Is Called Thinking?* published by Harper & Row, 1968, and *Zur Seinsfrage*.

Concerning the interpretation of Hegel's metaphysics, cf. my *Hegel's Concept of Experience*, in preparation for publication by Harper & Row.

The *Letter on Humanism*, which speaks everywhere only by implication, can become a possible stimulus to an explication of the matter of thinking only in retrospect from this publication and those cited here.

APPENDIX

IDENTITÄT UND DIFFERENZ

MARTIN HEIDEGGER

IDENTITÄT UND DIFFERENZ

Der Satz der Identität enthält den unveränderten Text eines
Vortrages, der beim fünfhundertjährigen Jubiläum der Uni-
versität Freiburg i.Br. zum Tag der Fakultäten am 27.Juni
1957 gehalten wurde.

Die onto-theo-logische Verfassung der Metaphysik gibt die
stellenweise überarbeitete Erörterung wieder, die eine Se-
minarübung des Wintersemesters 1956/57 über *Hegels*
«Wissenschaft der Logik» abschließt. Der Vortrag fand am
24.Februar 1957 in Todtnauberg statt.

Der Satz der Identität blickt voraus und blickt zurück: Voraus in den Bereich, von dem her das gesagt ist, was der Vortrag «Das Ding» erörtert (siehe Hinweise); zurück in den

Bereich der Wesensherkunft der Metaphysik, deren Verfassung durch die *Differenz* bestimmt ist.

Die Zusammengehörigkeit von *Identität und Differenz* wird in der vorliegenden Veröffentlichung als das zu Denkende gezeigt.

Inwiefern die Differenz dem Wesen der Identität entstammt, soll der Leser selbst finden, indem er auf den Einklang hört, der zwischen *Ereignis* und *Austrag* waltet.

Beweisen läßt sich in diesem Bereich nichts, aber weisen manches.

Todtnauberg, am 9. September 1957

DER SATZ DER IDENTITÄT

Der Satz der Identität lautet nach einer geläufigen Formel: A = A. Der Satz gilt als das oberste Denkgesetz. Diesem Satz versuchen wir für eine Weile nachzudenken. Denn wir möchten durch den Satz erfahren, was Identität ist.

Wenn das Denken, von einer Sache angesprochen, dieser nachgeht, kann es ihm geschehen, daß es sich unterwegs wandelt. Darum ist es ratsam, im folgenden auf den Weg zu achten, weniger auf den Inhalt. Beim Inhalt recht zu verweilen, verwehrt uns schon der Fortgang des Vortrages.

Was sagt die Formel A = A, in der man den Satz der Identität darzustellen pflegt? Die Formel nennt die Gleichheit von A und A. Zu einer Gleichung gehören wenigstens zwei. Ein A gleicht einem anderen. Will der Satz der Identität solches aussagen? Offenkundig nicht. Das Identische, lateinisch idem, heißt griechisch τὸ αὐτό. In unsere deutsche Sprache übersetzt, heißt τὸ αὐτό das Selbe. Wenn einer immerfort dasselbe sagt, z. B.: die Pflanze ist Pflanze, spricht er in einer Tautologie. Damit etwas das Selbe sein kann, genügt jeweils eines. Es bedarf nicht ihrer zwei wie bei der Gleichheit. Die Formel A = A spricht von Gleichheit. Sie nennt A nicht als dasselbe. Die geläufige Formel für den Satz der Identität verdeckt somit gerade das, was der Satz sagen möchte: A ist A, d. h. jedes A ist selber dasselbe.

Während wir das Identische in dieser Weise umschreiben, klingt ein altes Wort an, wodurch Platon das Identische vernehmlich macht, ein Wort, das auf ein noch älteres zurückdeutet. Platon spricht im Dialog Sophistes 254 d von στάσις und κίνησις, von Stillstand und Umschlag. Platon läßt an dieser Stelle den Fremdling sagen: οὐκοῦν αὐτῶν ἕκαστον τοῖν μὲν δυοῖν ἕτερόν ἐστιν, αὐτὸ δ'ἑαυτῷ ταὐτόν.

«Nun ist doch von ihnen jedes der beiden ein anderes, selber jedoch ihm selbst dasselbe.» Platon sagt nicht nur: ἕκαστον αὐτὸ ταὐτόν, «jedes selber dasselbe», sondern: ἕκαστον ἑαυτῷ ταὐτόν, «jedes selber ihm selbst dasselbe».

Der Dativ ἑαυτῷ bedeutet: jedes etwas selber ist ihm selbst

86

zurückgegeben, jedes selber ist dasselbe – nämlich für es selbst mit ihm selbst. Unsere deutsche Sprache verschenkt hier gleich wie die griechische den Vorzug, das Identische mit demselben Wort, aber dies in einer Fuge seiner verschiedenen Gestalten zu verdeutlichen.

Die gemäßere Formel für den Satz der Identität A ist A sagt demnach nicht nur: Jedes A ist selber dasselbe, sie sagt vielmehr: Mit ihm selbst ist jedes A selber dasselbe. In der Selbigkeit liegt die Beziehung des «mit», also eine Vermittelung, eine Verbindung, eine Synthesis: die Einung in eine Einheit.

Daher kommt es, daß die Identität durch die Geschichte des abendländischen Denkens hindurch im Charakter der Einheit erscheint. Aber diese Einheit ist keineswegs die fade Leere dessen, was, in sich beziehungslos, anhaltend auf einem Einerlei beharrt. Bis jedoch die in der Identität waltende, frühzeitig schon anklingende Beziehung desselben mit ihm selbst als diese Vermittelung entschieden und geprägt zum Vorschein kommt, bis gar eine Unterkunft gefunden wird für dieses Hervorscheinen der Vermittelung innerhalb der Identität, braucht das abendländische Denken mehr denn zweitausend Jahre. Denn erst die Philosophie des spekulativen Idealismus stiftet, vorbereitet von Leibniz und Kant, durch

Fichte, Schelling und Hegel dem in sich synthetischen Wesen der Identität eine Unterkunft. Diese kann hier nicht gezeigt werden. Nur eines ist zu behalten: Seit der Epoche des spekulativen Idealismus bleibt es dem Denken untersagt, die Einheit der Identität als das bloße Einerlei vorzustellen und von der in der Einheit waltenden Vermittelung abzusehen. Wo solches geschieht, wird die Identität nur abstrakt vorgestellt. Auch in der verbesserten Formel «A ist A» kommt allein die abstrakte Identität zum Vorschein. Kommt es dahin? Sagt der Satz der Identität etwas über die Identität aus? Nein, wenigstens nicht unmittelbar. Der Satz setzt vielmehr schon voraus, was Identität heißt und wohin sie gehört. Wie erlangen wir eine Auskunft über diese Voraussetzung? Der Satz der Identität gibt sie uns, wenn wir sorgsam auf seinen Grundton hören, ihm nachsinnen, statt nur leichtsinnig die Formel «A ist A» daherzusagen. Eigentlich lautet sie: A *ist* A. Was hören wir? In diesem «ist» sagt der Satz, wie jegliches Seiende ist, nämlich: Es selber mit ihm selbst dasselbe. Der Satz der Identität spricht vom Sein des Seienden. Als ein Gesetz des Denkens gilt der Satz nur, insofern er ein Gesetz des Seins ist, das lautet: Zu jedem Seienden als solchem gehört die Identität, die Einheit mit ihm selbst.

Was der Satz der Identität, aus seinem Grundton gehört, aussagt, ist genau das, was das gesamte abendländisch-europäische Denken denkt, nämlich dies: Die Einheit der Identität bildet einen Grundzug im Sein des Seienden. Überall, wo und wie wir uns zum Seienden jeglicher Art verhalten, finden wir uns von der Identität angesprochen. Spräche dieser Anspruch nicht, dann vermöchte es das Seiende niemals, in seinem Sein zu erscheinen. Demzufolge gäbe es auch keine Wissenschaft. Denn wäre ihr nicht zum voraus jeweils die Selbigkeit ihres Gegenstandes verbürgt, die Wissenschaft könnte nicht sein, was sie ist. Durch diese Bürgschaft sichert sich die Forschung die Möglichkeit ihrer Arbeit. Gleichwohl bringt die Leitvorstellung der Identität des Gegenstandes den Wissenschaften nie einen greifbaren Nutzen. Demnach beruht das Erfolgreiche und Fruchtbare der wissenschaftlichen Erkenntnis überall auf etwas Nutzlosem. Der Anspruch der Identität des Gegenstandes *spricht*, gleichviel ob die Wissenschaften diesen Anspruch hören oder nicht, ob sie das Gehörte in den Wind schlagen oder sich dadurch bestürzen lassen.

Der Anspruch der Identität spricht aus dem Sein des Seienden. Wo nun aber das Sein des Seienden im abendländischen

Denken am frühesten und eigens zur Sprache kommt, nämlich bei Parmenides, da spricht τὸ αὐτό, das Identische, in einem fast übermäßigen Sinne. Einer der Sätze des Parmenides lautet:

τὸ γὰρ αὐτὸ νοεῖν ἐστίν τε καὶ εἶναι.

«Das Selbe nämlich ist Vernehmen (Denken) sowohl als auch Sein.»

Hier wird Verschiedenes, Denken und Sein, als das Selbe gedacht. Was sagt dies? Etwas völlig anderes im Vergleich zu dem, was wir sonst als die Lehre der Metaphysik kennen, daß die Identität zum Sein gehört. Parmenides sagt: Das Sein gehört in eine Identität. Was heißt hier Identität? Was sagt im Satz des Parmenides das Wort τὸ αὐτό, das Selbe? Parmenides gibt uns auf diese Frage keine Antwort. Er stellt uns vor ein Rätsel, dem wir nicht ausweichen dürfen. Wir müssen anerkennen: In der Frühzeit des Denkens spricht, längst bevor es zu einem Satz der Identität kommt, die Identität selber und zwar in einem Spruch, der verfügt: Denken und Sein gehören in das Selbe und aus diesem Selben zusammen.

Unversehens haben wir jetzt τὸ αὐτό, das Selbe, schon gedeutet. Wir legen die Selbigkeit als Zusammengehörigkeit aus. Es liegt nahe, diese Zusammengehörigkeit im Sinne der später gedachten und allgemein bekannten Identität vorzustellen. Was könnte uns daran hindern? Nichts Geringeres als der Satz selbst, den wir bei Parmenides lesen. Denn er sagt anderes, nämlich: Sein gehört – mit dem Denken – in das Selbe. Das Sein ist von einer Identität her als ein Zug dieser Identität bestimmt. Dagegen wird die später in der Metaphysik gedachte Identität als ein Zug im Sein vorgestellt. Also können wir von dieser metaphysisch vorgestellten Identität aus nicht jene bestimmen wollen, die Parmenides nennt.

Die Selbigkeit von Denken und Sein, die im Satz des Parmenides spricht, kommt weiter her als die von der Metaphysik aus dem Sein als dessen Zug bestimmte Identität.

Das Leitwort im Satz des Parmenides, τὸ αὐτό, das Selbe, bleibt dunkel. Wir lassen es dunkel. Wir lassen uns aber zugleich von dem Satz, an dessen Beginn es steht, einen Wink geben.

Inzwischen haben wir aber die Selbigkeit von Denken und Sein schon als die Zusammengehörigkeit beider festgelegt. Dies war voreilig, vielleicht notgedrungen. Wir müssen das Voreilige rückgängig machen. Wir können dies auch, insofern wir die genannte Zusammengehörigkeit nicht für die endgültige und gar allein maßgebende Auslegung der Selbigkeit von Denken und Sein halten.

Denken wir das *Zusammen*gehören nach der Gewohnheit, dann wird, was schon die Betonung des Wortes andeutet, der Sinn des Gehörens vom Zusammen, d. h. von dessen Einheit her bestimmt. In diesem Fall heißt «gehören» soviel wie: zugeordnet und eingeordnet in die Ordnung eines Zusammen, eingerichtet in die Einheit eines Mannigfaltigen, zusammengestellt zur Einheit des Systems, vermittelt durch die einigende Mitte einer maßgebenden Synthesis. Die Philosophie stellt dieses Zusammengehören als nexus und connexio vor, als die notwendige Verknüpfung des einen mit dem anderen.

Indes läßt sich das Zusammengehören auch als Zusammen*gehören* denken. Dies will sagen: Das Zusammen wird jetzt aus dem Gehören bestimmt. Hier bleibt allerdings zu fragen, was dann «gehören» besage und wie sich aus ihm erst das ihm eigene Zusammen bestimme. Die Antwort auf diese Fragen liegt uns näher als wir meinen, aber sie liegt nicht auf der Hand. Genug, wenn wir jetzt durch diesen Hinweis auf die Möglichkeit merken, das Gehören nicht mehr aus der Einheit des Zusammen vorzustellen, sondern dieses Zusammen aus dem Gehören her zu erfahren. Allein, erschöpft sich der Hinweis auf diese Möglichkeit nicht in einem leeren

Wortspiel, das etwas erkünstelt, dem jeder Anhalt in einem nachprüfbaren Sachverhalt fehlt?

So sieht es aus, bis wir schärfer zusehen und die Sache sprechen lassen.

Der Gedanke an ein Zusammengehören im Sinne des Zusammen*gehörens* entspringt aus dem Hinblick auf einen Sachverhalt, der schon genannt wurde. Er ist freilich seiner Einfachheit wegen schwer im Blick zu behalten. Indessen kommt uns dieser Sachverhalt sogleich näher, wenn wir folgendes beachten: Bei der Erläuterung des Zusammengehörens als Zusammen*gehören* hatten wir schon, nach dem Wink des Parmenides, Denken sowohl als auch Sein im Sinn, also das, was im Selben zueinandergehört.

Verstehen wir das Denken als die Auszeichnung des Menschen, dann besinnen wir uns auf ein Zusammen*gehören*, das Mensch und Sein betrifft. Im Nu sehen wir uns von den Fragen bedrängt: Was heißt Sein? Wer oder was ist der Mensch? Jedermann sieht leicht: Ohne die zureichende Beantwortung dieser Fragen fehlt uns der Boden, auf dem wir etwas Verläßliches über das Zusammen*gehören* von Mensch und Sein ausmachen können. Solange wir jedoch auf diese Weise fragen, bleiben wir in den Versuch gebannt, das Zusammen von Mensch und Sein als eine Zuordnung vorzustellen und diese entweder vom Menschen her oder vom Sein aus einzurichten und zu erklären. Hierbei bilden die überlieferten Begriffe vom Menschen und vom Sein die Fußpunkte für die Zuordnung beider.

Wie wäre es, wenn wir, statt unentwegt nur eine Zusammenordnung beider vorzustellen, um ihre Einheit herzustellen, einmal darauf achteten, ob und wie in diesem Zusammen vor allem ein Zu-einander-Gehören im Spiel ist? Nun besteht sogar die Möglichkeit, das Zusammengehören von Mensch und Sein schon in den überlieferten Bestimmungen ihres Wesens, wenngleich nur aus der Ferne zu erblicken. Inwiefern?

Offenbar ist der Mensch etwas Seiendes. Als dieses gehört er wie der Stein, der Baum, der Adler in das Ganze des Seins. Gehören heißt hier noch: eingeordnet in das Sein. Aber das Auszeichnende des Menschen beruht darin, daß er als das denkende Wesen, offen dem Sein, vor dieses gestellt ist, auf das Sein bezogen bleibt und ihm so entspricht. Der Mensch *ist* eigentlich dieser Bezug der Entsprechung, und er ist nur dies. «Nur» – dies meint keine Beschränkung, sondern ein Übermaß. Im Menschen waltet ein Gehören zum Sein, welches Gehören auf das Sein hört, weil es diesem übereignet ist.

Und das Sein? Denken wir das Sein nach seinem anfänglichen Sinne als Anwesen. Das Sein west den Menschen weder beiläufig noch ausnahmsweise an. Sein west und währt nur, indem es durch seinen Anspruch den Menschen an-geht. Denn erst der Mensch, offen für das Sein, läßt dieses als Anwesen ankommen. Solches An-wesen braucht das Offene einer Lichtung und bleibt so durch dieses Brauchen dem Menschenwesen übereignet. Dies besagt keineswegs, das Sein werde erst und nur durch den Menschen gesetzt. Dagegen wird deutlich:

Mensch und Sein sind einander übereignet. Sie gehören einander. Aus diesem nicht näher bedachten Zueinandergehören haben Mensch und Sein allererst diejenigen Wesensbestimmungen empfangen, in denen sie durch die Philosophie metaphysisch begriffen werden.

Dieses vorwaltende Zusammen*gehören* von Mensch und Sein verkennen wir hartnäckig, solange wir alles nur in Ordnungen und Vermittlungen, sei es mit oder ohne Dialektik, vorstellen. Wir finden dann immer nur Verknüpfungen, die entweder vom Sein oder vom Menschen her geknüpft sind und das Zusammengehören von Mensch und Sein als Verflechtung darstellen.

Wir kehren noch nicht in das Zusammen*gehören* ein. Wie aber kommt es zu einer solchen Einkehr? Dadurch, daß wir uns von der Haltung des vorstellenden Denkens absetzen. Dieses Sichabsetzen ist ein Satz im Sinne eines Sprunges. Er springt ab, nämlich weg aus der geläufigen Vorstellung vom Menschen als dem animal rationale, das in der Neuzeit zum Subjekt für seine Objekte geworden ist. Der Absprung springt zugleich weg vom Sein. Dieses wird jedoch seit der Frühzeit des abendländischen Denkens als der Grund ausgelegt, worin jedes Seiende als Seiendes gründet.

Wohin springt der Absprung, wenn er vom Grund abspringt? Springt er in einen Abgrund? Ja, solange wir den Sprung nur vorstellen und zwar im Gesichtskreis des metaphysischen Denkens. Nein, insofern wir springen und uns loslassen. Wohin? Dahin, wohin wir schon eingelassen sind: in das Gehören zum Sein. Das Sein selbst aber gehört zu uns; denn nur bei uns kann es als Sein wesen, d. h. an-wesen.

So wird denn, um das Zusammen*gehören* von Mensch und Sein eigens zu erfahren, ein Sprung nötig. Dieser Sprung ist das Jähe der brückenlosen Einkehr in jenes Gehören, das erst ein Zueinander von Mensch und Sein und damit die Konstellation beider zu vergeben hat. Der Sprung ist die jähe Einfahrt in den Bereich, aus dem her Mensch und Sein einander je schon in ihrem Wesen erreicht haben, weil beide aus einer Zureichung einander übereignet sind. Die Einfahrt in den Bereich dieser Übereignung stimmt und be-stimmt erst die Erfahrung des Denkens.

Seltsamer Sprung, der uns vermutlich den Einblick erbringt, daß wir uns noch nicht genügend dort aufhalten, wo wir eigentlich schon sind. Wo sind wir? In welcher Konstellation von Sein und Mensch?

Heute benötigen wir, so scheint es wenigstens, nicht mehr wie noch vor Jahren umständliche Hinweise, damit wir die Konstellation erblicken, aus der Mensch und Sein einander angehen. Es genügt, so möchte man meinen, das Wort Atomzeitalter zu nennen, um erfahren zu lassen, wie das Sein heute in der technischen Welt uns an-west. Aber dürfen wir denn die technische Welt ohne weiteres mit dem Sein in eins setzen? Offenbar nicht, auch dann nicht, wenn wir diese Welt als das Ganze vorstellen, worin Atomenergie, rechnende Planung des Menschen und Automatisierung zusammengeschlossen sind. Weshalb bringt ein so gearteter Hinweis auf die technische Welt, mag er diese noch so weitläufig abschildern, keineswegs schon die Konstellation von Sein und

Mensch in den Blick? Weil jede Analyse der Situation zu kurz denkt, insofern das erwähnte Ganze der technischen Welt zum voraus vom Menschen her als dessen Gemächte gedeutet wird. Das Technische, im weitesten Sinne und nach seinen vielfältigen Erscheinungen vorgestellt, gilt als der Plan, den der Mensch entwirft, welcher Plan den Menschen schließlich in die Entscheidung drängt, ob er zum Knecht seines Planes werden oder dessen Herr bleiben will.

Durch diese Vorstellung vom Ganzen der technischen Welt schraubt man alles auf den Menschen zurück und gelangt, wenn es hoch kommt, zur Forderung einer Ethik der technischen Welt. In dieser Vorstellung befangen, bestärkt man sich selber in der Meinung, die Technik sei nur eine Sache des Menschen. Man überhört den Anspruch des Seins, der im Wesen der Technik spricht.

Setzen wir uns endlich davon ab, das Technische nur technisch, d. h. vom Menschen und seinen Maschinen her vorzustellen. Achten wir auf den Anspruch, unter dem in unserem Zeitalter nicht nur der Mensch, sondern alles Seiende, Natur und Geschichte, hinsichtlich ihres Seins stehen.

Welchen Anspruch meinen wir? Unser ganzes Dasein findet sich überall – bald spielend, bald drangvoll, bald gehetzt, bald geschoben –, herausgefordert, sich auf das Planen und Berechnen von allem zu verlegen. Was spricht in dieser Herausforderung? Entspringt sie nur einer selbstgemachten Laune des Menschen? Oder geht uns dabei schon das Seiende selbst an, und zwar so, daß es uns auf seine Planbarkeit und Berechenbarkeit hin anspricht? Dann stünde also gar das Sein unter der Herausforderung, das Seiende im Gesichtskreis der Berechenbarkeit erscheinen zu lassen? In der Tat. Und nicht nur dies. Im selben Maße wie das Sein ist der Mensch herausgefordert, d. h. gestellt, das ihn angehende Seiende als den Bestand seines Planens und Rechnens sicherzustellen und dieses Bestellen ins Unabsehbare zu treiben.

Der Name für die Versammlung des Herausforderns, das Mensch und Sein einander so zu-stellt, daß sie sich wechselweise stellen, lautet: das Ge-Stell. Man hat sich an diesem Wortgebrauch gestoßen. Aber wir sagen statt «stellen» auch «setzen» und finden nichts dabei, daß wir das Wort Ge-setz gebrauchen. Warum also nicht auch Ge-Stell, wenn der Blick in den Sachverhalt dies verlangt?

Dasjenige, worin und woher Mensch und Sein in der technischen Welt einander an-gehen, spricht an in der Weise des Ge-Stells. Im wechselweisen Sichstellen von Mensch und

Sein hören wir den Anspruch, der die Konstellation unseres Zeitalters bestimmt. Das Ge-Stell geht uns überall unmittelbar an. Das Ge-Stell ist, falls wir jetzt noch so sprechen dürfen, seiender denn alle Atomenergien und alles Maschinenwesen, seiender als die Wucht der Organisation, Information und Automatisierung. Weil wir das, was Ge-Stell heißt, nicht mehr im Gesichtskreis des Vorstellens antreffen, der uns das Sein des Seienden als Anwesen denken läßt – das Ge-Stell geht uns nicht mehr an wie etwas Anwesendes –, deshalb ist es zunächst befremdlich. Befremdlich bleibt das Ge-Stell vor allem insofern, als es nicht ein Letztes ist, sondern selber uns erst Jenes zuspielt, was die Konstellation von Sein und Mensch eigentlich durchwaltet.

Das Zusammen*gehören* von Mensch und Sein in der Weise der wechselseitigen Herausforderung bringt uns bestürzend näher, daß und wie der Mensch dem Sein vereignet, das Sein aber dem Menschenwesen zugeeignet ist. Im Ge-Stell waltet ein seltsames Vereignen und Zueignen. Es gilt, dieses Eignen, worin Mensch und Sein einander ge-eignet sind, schlicht zu erfahren, d. h. einzukehren in das, was wir das *Ereignis* nennen. Das Wort Ereignis ist der gewachsenen Sprache entnommen. Er-eignen heißt ursprünglich: er-äugen, d.h. er-

blicken, im Blicken zu sich rufen, an-eignen. Das Wort Er-
eignis soll jetzt, aus der gewiesenen Sache her gedacht, als
Leitwort im Dienst des Denkens sprechen. Als so gedachtes
Leitwort läßt es sich sowenig übersetzen wie das griechische
Leitwort λόγος und das chinesische Tao. Das Wort Ereignis
meint hier nicht mehr das, was wir sonst irgendein Ge-
schehnis, ein Vorkommnis nennen. Das Wort ist jetzt als
Singulare tantum gebraucht. Was es nennt, ereignet sich nur
in der Einzahl, nein, nicht einmal mehr in einer Zahl, sondern einzig. Was wir im Ge-Stell als der Konstellation von Sein
und Mensch durch die moderne technische Welt erfahren, ist
ein *Vorspiel* dessen, was Er-eignis heißt. Dieses verharrt jedoch nicht notwendig in seinem Vorspiel. Denn im Er-eignis
spricht die Möglichkeit an, daß es das bloße Walten des Ge-
Stells in ein anfänglicheres Ereignen verwindet. Eine solche
Verwindung des Ge-Stells aus dem Er-eignis in dieses brächte
die ereignishafte, also niemals vom Menschen allein mach-
bare, Zurücknahme der technischen Welt aus ihrer Herrschaft
zur Dienstschaft innerhalb des Bereiches, durch den der
Mensch eigentlicher in das Er-eignis reicht.

Wohin hat der Weg geführt? Zur Einkehr unseres Denkens
in jenes Einfache, das wir im strengen Wortsinne das Er-

eignis nennen. Es scheint, als gerieten wir jetzt in die Gefahr, unser Denken allzu unbekümmert in etwas abgelegenes Allgemeines zu richten, während sich uns doch mit dem, was das Wort Er-eignis nennen möchte, nur das Nächste jenes Nahen unmittelbar zuspricht, darin wir uns schon aufhalten. Denn was könnte uns näher sein als das, was uns dem nähert, dem wir gehören, worin wir Gehörende sind, das Er-eignis?

Das Er-eignis ist der in sich schwingende Bereich, durch den Mensch und Sein einander in ihrem Wesen erreichen, ihr Wesendes gewinnen, indem sie jene Bestimmungen verlieren, die ihnen die Metaphysik geliehen hat.

Das Ereignis als Er-eignis denken, heißt, am Bau dieses in sich schwingenden Bereiches bauen. Das Bauzeug zu diesem in sich schwebenden Bau empfängt das Denken aus der Sprache. Denn die Sprache ist die zarteste, aber auch die anfälligste, alles verhaltende Schwingung im schwebenden Bau des Ereignisses. Insofern unser Wesen in die Sprache vereignet ist, wohnen wir im Ereignis.

Wir sind jetzt an eine Wegstelle gelangt, wo sich die zwar grobe aber unvermeidliche Frage aufdrängt: Was hat das Ereignis mit der Identität zu tun? Antwort: Nichts. Dagegen hat die Identität vieles, wenn nicht alles mit dem Ereignis zu tun.

Inwiefern? Wir antworten, indem wir den begangenen Weg mit wenigen Schritten zurückgehen.

Das Ereignis vereignet Mensch und Sein in ihr wesenhaftes Zusammen. Ein erstes, bedrängendes Aufblitzen des Ereignisses erblicken wir im Ge-Stell. Dieses macht das Wesen der modernen technischen Welt aus. Im Ge-Stell erblicken wir ein Zusammen*gehören* von Mensch und Sein, worin das Gehörenlassen erst die Art des Zusammen und dessen Einheit bestimmt. Das Geleit in die Frage nach einem Zusammengehören, darin das Gehören den Vorrang vor dem Zusammen hat, ließen wir uns durch den Satz des Parmenides geben: «Das Selbe nämlich ist Denken sowohl als auch Sein.» Die Frage nach dem Sinn dieses Selben ist die Frage nach dem Wesen der Identität. Die Lehre der Metaphysik stellt die Identität als einen Grundzug im Sein vor. Jetzt zeigt sich: Sein gehört mit dem Denken in eine Identität, deren Wesen aus jenem Zusammengehörenlassen stammt, das wir das Ereignis nennen. Das Wesen der Identität ist ein Eigentum des Er-eignisses.

Für den Fall, daß an dem Versuch, unser Denken in den Ort der Wesensherkunft der Identität zu weisen, etwas Haltbares sein könnte, was wäre dann aus dem Titel des Vortrages geworden? Der Sinn des Titels „Der Satz der Identität" hätte sich gewandelt.

Der Satz gibt sich zunächst in der Form eines Grundsatzes, der die Identität als einen Zug im Sein, d. h. im Grund des Seienden voraussetzt. Aus diesem Satz im Sinne einer Aussage ist unterwegs ein Satz geworden von der Art eines Sprunges, der sich vom Sein als dem Grund des Seienden absetzt und so in den Abgrund springt. Doch dieser Abgrund ist weder das leere Nichts noch eine finstere Wirrnis, sondern: das Er-eignis. Im Er-eignis schwingt das Wesen dessen, was als Sprache spricht, die einmal das Haus des Seins genannt wurde. Satz der Identität sagt jetzt: Ein Sprung, den das Wesen der Identität verlangt, weil es ihn braucht, wenn anders das Zusammen*gehören* von Mensch und Sein in das Wesenslicht des Ereignisses gelangen soll.

Unterwegs vom Satz als einer Aussage über die Identität zum Satz als Sprung in die Wesensherkunft der Identität hat sich das Denken gewandelt. Darum erblickt es, der Gegenwart entgegenblickend, über die Situation des Menschen hinweg die Konstellation von Sein und Mensch aus dem, was beide einander eignet, aus dem Er-eignis.

Gesetzt, die Möglichkeit warte uns entgegen, daß sich uns das

Ge-Stell, die wechselweise Herausforderung von Mensch und Sein in die Berechnung des Berechenbaren, als das Ereignis zuspricht, das Mensch und Sein erst in ihr Eigentliches enteignet, dann wäre ein Weg frei, auf dem der Mensch da-Seiende, das Ganze der modernen technischen Welt, Natur und Geschichte, allem zuvor ihr Sein, anfänglicher erfährt. So lange die Besinnung auf die Welt des Atomzeitalters bei allem Ernst der Verantwortung nur dahin drängt, aber auch nur dabei als dem Ziel sich beruhigt, die friedliche Nutzung der Atomenergie zu betreiben, so lange bleibt das Denken auf halbem Wege stehen. Durch diese Halbheit wird die technische Welt in ihrer metaphysischen Vorherrschaft weiterhin und erst recht gesichert.

Allein, wo ist entschieden, daß die Natur als solche für alle Zukunft die Natur der modernen Physik bleiben und die Geschichte sich nur als Gegenstand der Historie darstellen müsse? Zwar können wir die heutige technische Welt weder als Teufelswerk verwerfen, noch dürfen wir sie vernichten, falls sie dies nicht selber besorgt.

Wir dürfen aber noch weniger der Meinung nachhängen, die technische Welt sei von einer Art, die einen Absprung aus ihr schlechthin verwehre. Diese Meinung hält nämlich das

Aktuelle, von ihm besessen, für das allein Wirkliche. Diese Meinung ist allerdings phantastisch, nicht dagegen ein Vordenken, das dem entgegenblickt, was als Zuspruch des Wesens der Identität von Mensch und Sein auf uns zukommt.

Mehr denn zweitausend Jahre brauchte das Denken, um eine so einfache Beziehung wie die Vermittelung innerhalb der Identität eigens zu begreifen. Dürfen *wir* da meinen, die denkende Einkehr in die Wesensherkunft der Identität lasse sich an einem Tage bewerkstelligen? Gerade weil diese Einkehr einen Sprung verlangt, braucht sie ihre Zeit, die Zeit des Denkens, die eine andere ist als diejenige des Rechnens, das heute überall her an unserem Denken zerrt. Heute errechnet die Denkmaschine in einer Sekunde Tausende von Beziehungen. Sie sind trotz ihres technischen Nutzens wesenlos.

Was immer und wie immer wir zu denken versuchen, wir denken im Spielraum der Überlieferung. Sie waltet, wenn sie uns aus dem Nachdenken in ein Vordenken befreit, das kein Planen mehr ist.

Erst wenn wir uns denkend dem schon Gedachten zuwenden, werden wir verwendet für das noch zu Denkende.

DIE ONTO-THEO-LOGISCHE VERFASSUNG
DER METAPHYSIK

Dieses Seminar versuchte, ein Gespräch mit *Hegel* zu beginnen. Das Gespräch mit einem Denker kann nur von der Sache des Denkens handeln. «Sache» meint nach der gegebenen Bestimmung den Streitfall, das Strittige, das einzig für das Denken *der* Fall ist, der das Denken angeht. Der Streit aber dieses Strittigen wird keineswegs erst durch das Denken gleichsam vom Zaun gebrochen. Die Sache des Denkens ist das in sich Strittige eines Streites. Unser Wort Streit (ahd. strit) meint vornehmlich nicht die Zwietracht sondern die Bedrängnis. Die Sache des Denkens bedrängt das Denken in der Weise, daß sie das Denken erst zu seiner Sache und von dieser her zu ihm selbst bringt.

Für Hegel ist die Sache des Denkens: Das Denken als solches.

Damit wir diese Umgrenzung der Sache, nämlich das Denken als solches, nicht psychologisch und nicht erkenntnistheoretisch mißdeuten, müssen wir erläuternd beifügen: Das Denken als solches – in der entwickelten Fülle der Gedachtheit des Gedachten. Was hier Gedachtheit des Gedachten besagt, können wir nur von Kant her verstehen, vom Wesen des Transzendentalen aus, das Hegel jedoch absolut, und d. h. für ihn spekulativ, denkt. Darauf zielt Hegel ab, wenn er vom Denken des Denkens als solchem sagt, daß es «rein im Elemente des Denkens» entwickelt werde (Enc. Einleitung § 14). Mit einem knappen, aber nur schwer sachgerecht auszudenkenden Titel benannt, heißt dies: Die Sache des Denkens ist für Hegel «der Gedanke». Dieser aber ist, zu seiner höchsten Wesensfreiheit entfaltet, «die absolute Idee». Von ihr sagt Hegel gegen Ende der «Wissenschaft der Logik» (ed. Lass. Bd. II, 484): «die absolute Idee allein ist *Sein* unvergängliches *Leben, sich wissende Wahrheit,* und ist *alle Wahrheit*». So gibt denn Hegel selbst und ausdrücklich der Sache seines Denkens denjenigen Namen, der über der ganzen Sache des abendländischen Denkens steht, den Namen: *Sein.*

(Im Seminar wurde der mehrfältige und doch einheitliche Gebrauch des Wortes «Sein» erörtert. Sein besagt für Hegel

zunächst, aber *niemals nur*, die «unbestimmte Unmittel-
barkeit». Sein ist hier gesehen aus dem bestimmenden Ver-
mitteln, d. h. vom absoluten Begriff her und deshalb auf diesen hin. «Die Wahrheit des Seins ist das Wesen», d.h. die absolute Reflexion. Die Wahrheit des Wesens ist der Begriff im
Sinne des un-endlichen Sichwissens. Sein ist das absolute
Sichdenken des Denkens. Das absolute Denken allein ist die
Wahrheit des Seins, «ist» Sein. Wahrheit heißt hier überall: die
ihrer selbst gewisse Gewußtheit des Wißbaren als solchen.)

Hegel denkt jedoch die Sache seines Denkens sachgemäß zugleich in einem Gespräch mit der voraufgegangenen Geschichte des Denkens. Hegel ist der erste, der so denken
kann und muß. Hegels Verhältnis zur Geschichte der Philosophie ist das spekulative und nur als dieses ein geschichtliches.
Der Charakter der Bewegung der Geschichte ist ein Geschehen im Sinne des dialektischen Prozesses. Hegel schreibt
(Enc. § 14): «Dieselbe Entwickelung des Denkens, welche in
der Geschichte der Philosophie dargestellt wird, wird in der
Philosophie selbst dargestellt, aber befreit von jener geschichtlichen Äußerlichkeit, *rein im Elemente des Denkens.*»

Wir stutzen und stocken. Die Philosophie selbst und die Geschichte der Philosophie sollen nach Hegels eigenem Wort im

Verhältnis der Äußerlichkeit stehen. Aber die von Hegel gedachte Äußerlichkeit ist keineswegs äußerlich in dem groben Sinne des bloß Oberflächlichen und Gleichgültigen. Äußerlichkeit besagt hier das Außerhalb, darin alle Geschichte und jeder wirkliche Verlauf gegenüber der Bewegung der absoluten Idee sich aufhält. Die erläuterte Äußerlichkeit der Geschichte im Verhältnis zur Idee ergibt sich als Folge der Selbstentäußerung der Idee. Die Äußerlichkeit ist selbst eine dialektische Bestimmung. Man bleibt daher weit hinter dem eigentlichen Gedanken Hegels zurück, wenn man feststellt, Hegel habe in der Philosophie das historische Vorstellen und das systematische Denken zu einer Einheit gebracht. Denn für Hegel handelt es sich weder um Historie, noch um das System im Sinne eines Lehrgebäudes.

Was sollen diese Bemerkungen über die Philosophie und deren Verhältnis zur Geschichte? Sie möchten andeuten, daß die Sache des Denkens für Hegel in sich geschichtlich ist, dies jedoch im Sinne des Geschehens. Dessen Prozeßcharakter wird durch die Dialektik des Seins bestimmt. Die Sache des Denkens ist für Hegel das Sein als das sich selbst denkende Denken, welches Denken erst im Prozeß seiner spekulativen Entwicklung zu sich selbst kommt und somit Stufen der je verschieden entwickelten und daher zuvor notwendig unentwickelten Gestalten durchläuft.

Erst aus der so erfahrenen Sache des Denkens entspringt für Hegel eine eigentümliche Maxime, die Maßgabe für die Art und Weise, wie er mit den voraufgegangenen Denkern spricht. Wenn wir also ein denkendes Gespräch mit Hegel versuchen, dann müssen wir mit ihm nicht nur von derselben Sache, sondern von derselben Sache in derselben Weise sprechen. Allein das Selbe ist nicht das Gleiche. Im Gleichen verschwindet die Verschiedenheit. Im Selben erscheint die Verschiedenheit. Sie erscheint um so bedrängender, je entschiedener ein Denken von derselben Sache auf dieselbe Weise angegangen wird. Hegel denkt das Sein des Seienden spekulativ-geschichtlich. Insofern nun aber Hegels Denken in eine Epoche der Geschichte gehört (dies meint beileibe nicht zum Vergangenen), versuchen wir, das von Hegel gedachte Sein auf dieselbe Weise, d. h. geschichtlich zu denken.

Bei seiner Sache kann das Denken nur dadurch bleiben, daß es im Dabei-bleiben jeweils sachlicher, daß ihm dieselbe Sache strittiger wird. Auf diese Weise verlangt die Sache vom Denken, daß es die Sache in ihrem Sachverhalt aushalte, ihm durch eine Entsprechung standhalte, indem es die Sache zu ihrem Austrag bringt. Das bei seiner Sache bleibende Denken muß, wenn diese Sache das Sein ist, sich auf den Austrag des Seins einlassen. Demgemäß sind wir daran gehalten, im Gespräch mit Hegel und für dieses zum voraus die Selbigkeit derselben Sache deutlicher zu machen. Dies verlangt nach dem Gesagten, mit der Verschiedenheit der Sache des Denkens zugleich die Verschiedenheit des Geschichtlichen im Gespräch mit der Geschichte der Philosophie ans Licht zu heben. Eine solche Verdeutlichung muß hier notgedrungen kurz und umrißweise ausfallen.

Wir beachten zum Zwecke einer Verdeutlichung der Verschiedenheit, die zwischen dem Denken Hegels und dem von uns versuchten Denken obwaltet, dreierlei.

Wir fragen:

1. Welches ist dort und hier die Sache des Denkens?

2. Welches ist dort und hier die Maßgabe für das Gespräch mit der Geschichte des Denkens?

3. Welches ist dort und hier der Charakter dieses Gespräches?

Zur ersten Frage:

Für Hegel ist die Sache des Denkens das Sein hinsichtlich der Gedachtheit des Seienden im absoluten Denken und als dieses.

Für uns ist die Sache des Denkens das Selbe, somit das Sein, aber das Sein hinsichtlich seiner Differenz zum Seienden. Noch schärfer gefaßt: Für Hegel ist die Sache des Denkens der Gedanke als der absolute Begriff. Für uns ist die Sache des Denkens, vorläufig benannt, die Differenz *als* Differenz.

Zur zweiten Frage:

Für Hegel lautet die Maßgabe für das Gespräch mit der Geschichte der Philosophie: Eingehen in die Kraft und den Umkreis des von den früheren Denkern Gedachten. Nicht zufällig stellt Hegel seine Maxime im Zuge eines Gespräches mit Spinoza und vor einem Gespräch mit Kant heraus (Wissenschaft der Logik, III. Buch, Lasson Bd. II, S. 216 ff). Bei Spinoza findet Hegel den vollendeten «Standpunkt der Substanz», der jedoch nicht der höchste sein kann, weil das Sein noch nicht ebensosehr und entschieden von Grund aus als sich denkendes Denken gedacht ist. Das Sein hat sich als Substanz und Substanzialität noch nicht zum Subjekt in seiner absoluten Subjektität entfaltet. Gleichwohl spricht Spinoza das gesamte Denken des deutschen Idealismus immer neu an und versetzt es zugleich in den Widerspruch, weil er das Denken mit dem Absoluten anfangen läßt. Dagegen ist der Weg Kants ein anderer und für das Denken des absoluten

Idealismus und für die Philosophie überhaupt noch weit entscheidender als das System Spinozas. Hegel sieht in Kants Gedanken der ursprünglichen Synthesis der Apperception «eines der tiefsten Prinzipien für die spekulative Entwicklung» (a. a. O. S. 227). Die jeweilige Kraft der Denker findet Hegel in dem von ihnen Gedachten, insofern es als jeweilige Stufe in das absolute Denken aufgehoben werden kann. Dieses ist nur dadurch absolut, daß es sich in seinem dialektisch-spekulativen Prozeß bewegt und dafür die Stufung verlangt.

Für uns ist die Maßgabe für das Gespräch mit der geschichtlichen Überlieferung dieselbe, insofern es gilt, in die Kraft des früheren Denkens einzugehen. Allein wir suchen die Kraft nicht im schon Gedachten, sondern in einem Ungedachten, von dem her das Gedachte seinen Wesensraum empfängt. Aber das schon Gedachte erst bereitet das noch Ungedachte, das immer neu in seinen Überfluß einkehrt. Die Maßgabe des Ungedachten führt nicht zum Einbezug des vormals Gedachten in eine immer noch höhere und es überholende Entwicklung und Systematik, sondern sie verlangt die Freilassung des überlieferten Denkens in sein noch aufgespartes Gewesenes. Dies durchwaltet anfänglich die Überlieferung, west ihr stets voraus, ohne doch eigens und als das Anfangende gedacht zu sein.

Zur dritten Frage:

Für Hegel hat das Gespräch mit der voraufgegangenen Geschichte der Philosophie den Charakter der Aufhebung, d. h. des vermittelnden Begreifens im Sinne der absoluten Begründung.

Für uns ist der Charakter des Gespräches mit der Geschichte des Denkens nicht mehr die Aufhebung, sondern der Schritt zurück.

Die Aufhebung führt in den überhöhend-versammelnden Bezirk der absolut gesetzten Wahrheit im Sinne der vollständig entfalteten Gewißheit des sich wissenden Wissens. Der Schritt zurück weist in den bisher übersprungenen Bereich, aus dem her das Wesen der Wahrheit allererst denkwürdig wird.

Nach dieser knappen Kennzeichnung der Verschiedenheit des Hegelschen Denkens und des unsrigen hinsichtlich der Sache, hinsichtlich der Maßgabe und des Charakters eines Gespräches mit der Geschichte des Denkens versuchen wir, das begonnene Gespräch mit Hegel um ein Geringes deutlicher in Gang zu bringen. Dies besagt: Wir wagen einen Versuch mit dem Schritt zurück. Der Titel «Schritt zurück» legt mehrfache Mißdeutungen nahe. «Schritt zurück» meint nicht einen vereinzelten Denkschritt, sondern die Art der Bewegung des Denkens und einen langen Weg. Insofern der Schritt zurück den Charakter unseres Gespräches mit der Geschichte des abendländischen Denkens bestimmt, führt das Denken aus dem in der Philosophie bisher Gedachten in gewisser Weise heraus. Das Denken tritt vor seiner Sache, dem Sein, zurück und bringt so das Gedachte in ein Gegenüber, darin wir das Ganze dieser Geschichte erblicken und zwar hinsichtlich dessen, was die Quelle dieses ganzen Denkens ausmacht, indem sie ihm überhaupt den Bezirk seines Aufenthaltes bereitstellt. Dies ist im Unterschied zu Hegel nicht ein überkommenes, schon gestelltes Problem, sondern das durch diese Geschichte des Denkens hindurch überall Ungefragte. Wir benennen es vorläufig und unvermeidlich in der Sprache der Überlieferung. Wir sprechen von der *Differenz* zwischen dem Sein und dem Seienden. Der Schritt zurück geht vom Ungedachten, von der Differenz als solcher, in das zu-Denkende. Das ist die *Vergessenheit* der Differenz. Die hier zu denkende Vergessenheit ist die von der Λήϑη (Verbergung) her gedachte Verhüllung der Differenz als solcher, welche Verhüllung ihrerseits sich anfänglich entzogen hat. Die Vergessenheit gehört zur Differenz, weil diese jener zugehört. Die Vergessenheit befällt nicht erst die Differenz nachträglich zufolge einer Vergeßlichkeit des menschlichen Denkens.

Die Differenz von Seiendem und Sein ist der Bezirk, innerhalb dessen die Metaphysik, das abendländische Denken im Ganzen seines Wesens das sein kann, was sie ist. Der Schritt zurück bewegt sich daher aus der Metaphysik in das Wesen der Metaphysik. Die Bemerkung über Hegels Gebrauch des mehrdeutigen Leitwortes «Sein» läßt erkennen, daß die Rede von Sein und Seiendem sich niemals auf *eine* Epoche der Lichtungsgeschichte von «Sein» festlegen läßt. Die Rede vom «Sein» versteht diesen Namen auch nie im Sinne einer Gattung, unter deren leere Allgemeinheit die historisch vorgestellten Lehren vom Seienden als einzelne Fälle gehören. «Sein» spricht je und je geschicklich und deshalb durchwaltet von Überlieferung.

Der Schritt zurück aus der Metaphysik in ihr Wesen verlangt nun aber eine Dauer und Ausdauer, deren Maße wir nicht kennen. Nur das eine ist deutlich: Der Schritt bedarf einer Vorbereitung, die jetzt und hier gewagt werden muß;

dies jedoch angesichts des Seienden als solchen im Ganzen, wie es jetzt *ist* und sich zusehends eindeutiger zu zeigen beginnt. Was jetzt *ist,* wird durch die Herrschaft des Wesens der modernen Technik geprägt, welche Herrschaft sich bereits auf allen Gebieten des Lebens durch vielfältig benennbare Züge wie Funktionalisierung, Perfektion, Automatisation, Bürokratisierung, Information darstellt. So wie wir die Vorstellung vom Lebendigen Biologie nennen, kann die Darstellung und Ausformung des vom Wesen der Technik durchherrschten Seienden Technologie heißen. Der Ausdruck darf als Bezeichnung für die Metaphysik des Atomzeitalters dienen. Der Schritt zurück aus der Metaphysik in das Wesen der Metaphysik ist, von der Gegenwart her gesehen und aus dem Einblick in sie übernommen, der Schritt aus der Technologie und technologischen Beschreibung und Deutung des Zeitalters in das erst zu denkende *Wesen* der modernen Technik.

Mit diesem Hinweis sei die andere naheliegende Mißdeutung des Titels «Schritt zurück» ferngehalten, die Meinung nämlich, der Schritt zurück bestehe in einem historischen Rückgang zu den frühesten Denkern der abendländischen Philosophie. Das Wohin freilich, dahin der Schritt zurück uns lenkt, entfaltet und zeigt sich erst durch den Vollzug des Schrittes.

Wir wählten, um durch das Seminar einen Blick in das Ganze der Hegelschen Metaphysik zu gewinnen, als Notbehelf eine Erörterung des Stückes, mit dem das I. Buch der «Wissenschaft der Logik», «Die Lehre vom Sein», beginnt. Schon der Titel des Stückes gibt in jedem Wort genug zu denken. Er lautet: «*Womit muß der Anfang der Wissenschaft gemacht werden?*» Hegels Beantwortung der Frage besteht in dem Nachweis, daß der Anfang «spekulativer Natur» ist. Dies sagt: Der Anfang ist weder etwas Unmittelbares noch etwas Vermitteltes. Diese Natur des Anfanges versuchten wir in einem spekulativen Satz zu sagen: «Der Anfang ist das Resultat.» Dies besagt nach der dialektischen Mehrdeutigkeit des «ist» mehrfaches. Einmal dies: Der Anfang ist – das resultare beim Wort genommen – der Rückprall aus der Vollendung der dialektischen Bewegung des sich denkenden Denkens. Die Vollendung dieser Bewegung, die absolute Idee, ist das geschlossen entfaltete Ganze, die Fülle des Seins. Der Rückprall aus dieser Fülle ergibt die Leere des Seins. Mit ihr muß in der Wissenschaft (dem absoluten, sich wissenden Wissen) der Anfang gemacht werden. Anfang und Ende der Bewegung, dem zuvor diese selber, bleibt überall das Sein. Es west als die in sich kreisende Bewegung von der Fülle in die äußerste Entäußerung und von dieser in die sich vollendende Fülle. Die Sache des Denkens ist somit für Hegel das sich denkende Denken als das in sich kreisende Sein. In der nicht nur berechtigten, sondern notwendigen Umkehrung lautet der spekulative Satz über den Anfang: «Das Resultat ist der Anfang.» Mit dem Resultat muß, insofern aus ihm der Anfang resultiert, eigentlich angefangen werden.

Dies sagt das Selbe wie die Bemerkung, die Hegel im Stück über den Anfang gegen Schluß beiläufig und in Klammern einfügt (Lass. I, 63): «(und das unbestrittenste Recht hätte *Gott,* daß mit ihm der Anfang gemacht werde)». Gemäß der Titelfrage des Stückes handelt es sich um den «Anfang der Wissenschaft». Wenn sie mit Gott den Anfang machen muß, ist sie die Wissenschaft von Gott: Theologie. Dieser Name spricht hier in seiner späteren Bedeutung. Darnach ist die Theo-logie die Aussage des vorstellenden Denkens über Gott. Zunächst meint θεόλογος, θεολογία das mythisch-dichtende Sagen von den Göttern ohne Beziehung auf eine Glaubenslehre und eine kirchliche Doktrin.

Weshalb ist «die Wissenschaft», so lautet seit Fichte der Name für die Metaphysik, weshalb ist die Wissenschaft Theologie? Antwort: Weil die Wissenschaft die systematische Entwicklung des Wissens ist, als welches sich das Sein des Seienden selbst weiß und so wahrhaft ist. Der schulmäßige, im Übergang vom Mittelalter zur Neuzeit auftauchende Titel für die Wissenschaft vom Sein, d. h. vom Seienden als solchem im allgemeinen, lautet: Ontosophie oder Ontologie. Nun ist aber die abendländische Metaphysik seit ihrem Beginn bei den Griechen und noch ungebunden an diese Titel zumal Ontologie und Theologie. In der Antrittsvorlesung «Was ist Metaphysik?» (1929) wird daher die Metaphysik als die Frage nach dem Seienden als solchem *und* im Ganzen bestimmt. Die Ganzheit dieses Ganzen ist die Einheit des Seienden, die als der hervorbringende Grund einigt. Für den, der lesen kann, heißt dies: Die Metaphysik ist Onto-Theo-Logie. Wer die Theologie, sowohl diejenige des christlichen Glaubens als auch diejenige der Philosophie, aus gewachsener Herkunft erfahren hat, zieht es heute vor, im Bereich des Denkens von Gott zu schweigen. Denn der onto-theologische Charakter der Metaphysik ist für das Denken fragwürdig geworden, nicht auf Grund irgendeines Atheismus, sondern aus der Erfahrung eines Denkens, dem sich in der Onto-Theo-Logie die noch *ungedachte* Einheit des Wesens der Metaphysik gezeigt hat. Dieses Wesen der Metaphysik bleibt indes immer noch das Denkwürdigste für das Denken, solange es das Gespräch mit seiner geschickhaften Überlieferung nicht willkürlich und darum unschicklich abbricht.

In der 5. Auflage von «Was ist Metaphysik?» (1949) gibt die zugefügte Einleitung den ausdrücklichen Hinweis auf das onto-theologische Wesen der Metaphysik (S. 17 f., 7. Aufl. S. 18 f.). Indessen wäre es voreilig zu behaupten, die Metaphysik sei Theologie, weil sie Ontologie sei. Zuvor wird man sagen: Die Metaphysik ist deshalb Theologie, ein Aussagen über Gott, weil der Gott in die Philosophie kommt. So verschärft sich die Frage nach dem onto-theologischen Charakter der Metaphysik zur Frage: Wie kommt der Gott in die Philosophie, nicht nur in die neuzeitliche, sondern in die Philosophie als solche? Die Frage läßt sich nur beantworten, wenn sie zuvor als Frage hinreichend entfaltet ist.

Die Frage: Wie kommt der Gott in die Philosophie? können wir nur dann sachgerecht durchdenken, wenn sich dabei dasjenige genügend aufgehellt hat, *wohin* denn der Gott kommen soll – die Philosophie selbst. Solange wir die Geschichte der Philosophie nur historisch absuchen, werden wir überall finden, daß der Gott in sie gekommen ist. Gesetzt aber, daß die Philosophie als Denken das freie, von sich aus vollzogene

Sicheinlassen auf das Seiende als solches ist, dann kann der Gott nur insofern in die Philosophie gelangen, als diese von sich aus, ihrem Wesen nach, verlangt und bestimmt, daß und wie der Gott in sie komme. Die Frage: Wie kommt der Gott in die Philosophie? fällt darum auf die Frage zurück: Woher stammt die onto-theologische Wesensverfassung der Metaphysik? Die so gestellte Frage übernehmen, heißt jedoch, den Schritt zurück vollziehen.

In diesem Schritt bedenken wir jetzt die Wesensherkunft der onto-theologischen Struktur aller Metaphysik. Wir fragen: Wie kommt der Gott und ihm entsprechend die Theologie und mit ihr der onto-theologische Grundzug in die Metaphysik? Wir stellen diese Frage in einem Gespräch mit dem Ganzen der Geschichte der Philosophie. Wir fragen aber zugleich aus dem besonderen Blick auf Hegel. Dies veranlaßt uns, zuvor etwas Seltsames zu bedenken.

Hegel denkt das Sein in seiner leersten Leere, also im Allgemeinsten. Er denkt das Sein zugleich in seiner vollendet vollkommenen Fülle. Gleichwohl nennt er die spekulative Philosophie, d. h. die eigentliche Philosophie, nicht Onto-Theologie, sondern «Wissenschaft der Logik». Mit dieser Namengebung bringt Hegel etwas Entscheidendes zum Vorschein.

Man könnte freilich die Benennung der Metaphysik als «Logik» im Handumdrehen durch den Hinweis darauf erklären, daß doch für Hegel die Sache des Denkens «der Gedanke» sei, das Wort als Singulare tantum verstanden. Der Gedanke, das Denken ist offenkundig und nach altem Brauch das Thema der Logik. Gewiß. Aber ebenso unbestreitbar liegt fest, daß Hegel getreu der Überlieferung die Sache des Denkens im Seienden als solchem und im Ganzen, in der Bewegung des Seins von seiner Leere zu seiner entwickelten Fülle findet.

Wie kann jedoch «das Sein» überhaupt darauf verfallen, sich als «der Gedanke» darzustellen? Wie anders denn dadurch, daß das Sein als Grund vorgeprägt ist, das Denken jedoch – dieweilen es mit dem Sein zusammengehört – auf das Sein als Grund sich versammelt in der Weise des Ergründens und Begründens? Das Sein manifestiert sich als der Gedanke. Dies sagt: Das Sein des Seienden entbirgt sich als der sich selbst ergründende und begründende Grund. Der Grund, die Ratio sind nach ihrer Wesensherkunft: der Λόγος im Sinne des versammelnden Vorliegenlassens: das Ἕν Πάντα. So ist denn für Hegel in Wahrheit «die Wissenschaft», d. h. die Metaphysik, nicht deshalb «Logik», weil die Wissenschaft das Denken zum Thema hat, sondern weil die Sache des Denkens das *Sein* bleibt, dieses jedoch seit der Frühe seiner Entbergung im Gepräge des Λόγος, des gründenden Grundes das Denken als Begründen in seinen Anspruch nimmt. Die Metaphysik denkt das Seiende als solches, d. h. im Allgemeinen. Die Metaphysik denkt das Seiende als solches, d. h. im Ganzen. Die Metaphysik denkt das Sein des Seienden sowohl in der ergründenden Einheit des Allgemeinsten, d. h. des überall Gleich-Gültigen, als auch in der begründenden Einheit der Allheit, d. h. des Höchsten über allem. So wird das Sein des Seienden als der gründende Grund vorausgedacht. Daher ist alle Metaphysik im Grunde vom Grund aus das Gründen, das vom Grund die Rechenschaft gibt, ihm Rede steht und ihn schließlich zur Rede stellt.

Wozu erwähnen wir dies? Damit wir die abgegriffenen Titel Ontologie, Theologie, Onto-Theologie in ihrem eigentlichen Schwergewicht erfahren. Zunächst allerdings und gewöhnlich nehmen sich die Titel Ontologie und Theologie aus wie andere bekannte auch: Psychologie, Biologie, Kosmologie, Archäologie. Die Endsilbe -logie meint ganz im Ungefähren und im Geläufigen, es handle sich um die Wissenschaft von der Seele, vom Lebendigen, vom Kosmos, von den Altertümern.

Aber in der -logie verbirgt sich nicht nur das Logische im Sinne des Folgerichtigen und überhaupt des Aussagemäßigen, das alles Wissen der Wissenschaften gliedert und bewegt, in Sicherheit bringt und mitteilt. Die -Logia ist jeweils das Ganze eines Begründungszusammenhanges, worin die Gegenstände der Wissenschaften im Hinblick auf ihren Grund vorgestellt, d. h. begriffen werden. Die Ontologie aber und die Theologie sind «Logien», insofern sie das Seiende als solches ergründen und im Ganzen begründen. Sie geben vom Sein ·als dem Grund des Seienden Rechenschaft. Sie stehen dem Λόγος Rede und sind in einem wesenhaften Sinne Λόγος-gemäß, d. h. die Logik des Λόγος. Demgemäß heißen sie genauer Onto-Logik und Theo-Logik. Die Metaphysik ist sachgemäßer und deutlicher gedacht: Onto-Theo-Logik.

Wir verstehen jetzt den Namen «Logik» in dem wesentlichen Sinne, der auch den von Hegel gebrauchten Titel einschließt und ihn so erst erläutert, nämlich als den Namen für dasjenige Denken, das überall das Seiende als solches im Ganzen vom Sein als dem Grund (Λόγος) her ergründet und begründet. Der Grundzug der Metaphysik heißt Onto-Theo-Logik. Somit wären wir in den Stand gesetzt zu erklären wie der Gott in die Philosophie kommt.

Inwieweit gelingt eine Erklärung? Insoweit wir beachten: Die Sache des Denkens ist das Seiende als solches, d. h. das Sein. Dieses zeigt sich in der Wesensart des Grundes. Demgemäß wird die Sache des Denkens, das Sein als der Grund, nur dann gründlich gedacht, wenn der Grund als der erste Grund, πρώτη ἀρχή, vorgestellt wird. Die ursprüngliche Sache des Denkens stellt sich als die Ur-Sache dar, als die causa prima, die dem begründenden Rückgang auf die ultima ratio, die letzte Rechenschaft, entspricht. Das Sein des Seienden wird im Sinne des Grundes gründlich nur als causa sui vorgestellt. Damit ist der metaphysische Begriff von Gott genannt. Die Metaphysik muß auf den Gott hinaus denken, weil die Sache des Denkens das Sein ist, dieses aber in vielfachen Weisen als Grund: als Λόγος, als ὑποκείμενον, als Substanz, als Subjekt west.

Diese Erklärung streift vermutlich etwas Richtiges, aber sie bleibt für die Erörterung des Wesens der Metaphysik durchaus unzureichend. Denn diese ist nicht nur Theo-Logik sondern auch Onto-Logik. Die Metaphysik ist vordem nicht nur das eine oder das andere *auch.* Vielmehr ist die Metaphysik Theo-Logik, weil sie Onto-Logik ist. Sie ist dieses, weil sie jenes ist. Die onto-theologische Wesensverfassung der Metaphysik kann weder von der Theologik noch von der Ontologik her erklärt werden, falls hier jemals ein Erklären dem genügt, was zu bedenken bleibt.

Noch ist nämlich ungedacht, aus welcher Einheit die Ontologik und Theologik zusammengehören, ungedacht die Herkunft dieser Einheit, ungedacht der Unterschied des Unterschiedenen, das sie einigt. Denn offenkundig handelt es sich nicht erst um einen Zusammenschluß zweier für sich bestehender Disziplinen der Metaphysik, sondern um die Einheit dessen, *was* in der Ontologik und Theologik befragt und *gedacht* wird: Das Seiende als solches im Allgemeinen und Ersten *in Einem mit* dem Seienden als solchem im Höchsten und Letzten. Die Einheit dieses Einen ist von solcher Art, daß das Letzte auf seine Weise das Erste begründet und das Erste auf seine Weise das Letzte. Die Verschiedenheit der beiden Weisen des Begründens fällt selber in den genannten, noch ungedachten Unterschied.

In der Einheit des Seienden als solchen im Allgemeinen und im Höchsten beruht die Wesensverfassung der Metaphysik.

Es gilt hier, die Frage nach dem onto-theologischen Wesen der Metaphysik zunächst nur als Frage zu erörtern. In den Ort, den die Frage nach der onto-theologischen Verfassung der Metaphysik erörtert, kann uns nur die Sache selbst weisen, dergestalt, daß wir die Sache des Denkens sachlicher zu denken versuchen. Die Sache des Denkens ist dem abendländischen Denken unter dem Namen «Sein» überliefert. Denken wir diese Sache um ein geringes sachlicher, achten wir sorgfältiger auf das Strittige in der Sache, dann zeigt sich: *Sein* heißt stets und überall: Sein *des Seienden*, bei welcher Wendung der Genitiv als genitivus obiectivus zu denken ist. *Seiendes* heißt stets und überall: Seiendes *des Seins*, bei welcher Wendung der Genitiv als genitivus subiectivus zu denken ist. Wir sprechen allerdings mit Vorbehalten von einem Genitiv in der Richtung auf Objekt und Subjekt; denn diese Titel Subjekt und Objekt sind ihrerseits schon einer Prägung des Seins entsprungen. Klar ist nur, daß es sich beim Sein des Seienden und beim Seienden des Seins jedesmal um eine Differenz handelt.

Sein denken wir demnach nur dann sachlich, wenn wir es in der Differenz mit dem Seienden denken und dieses in der Differenz mit dem Sein. So kommt die Differenz eigens in den Blick. Versuchen wir sie vorzustellen, dann finden wir uns sogleich dazu verleitet, die Differenz als eine Relation aufzufassen, die unser Vorstellen zum Sein und zum Seienden hinzugetan hat. Dadurch wird die Differenz zu einer Distinktion, zu einem Gemächte unseres Verstandes herabgesetzt.

Doch nehmen wir einmal an, die Differenz sei eine Zutat unseres Vorstellens, dann erhebt sich die Frage: eine Zutat wohinzu? Man antwortet: zum Seienden. Gut. Aber was heißt dies: «das Seiende»? Was heißt es anderes als: solches, das *ist?* So bringen wir denn die vermeintliche Zutat, die Vorstellung von der Differenz, beim Sein unter. Aber «Sein» sagt selber: Sein, das *Seiendes* ist. Wir treffen dort, wohin wir die Differenz als angebliche Zutat erst mitbringen sollen, immer schon Seiendes und Sein in ihrer Differenz an. Es ist hier wie im Grimmschen Märchen vom Hasen und Igel: «Ick bünn all hier». Nun könnte man mit diesem seltsamen Sachverhalt, daß Seiendes und Sein je schon aus der Differenz und in ihr vorgefunden werden, auf eine massive Weise verfahren und ihn so erklären: Unser vorstellendes Denken ist nun einmal so eingerichtet und beschaffen, daß es gleichsam über seinen Kopf hinweg und diesem Kopf entstammend überall zwischen dem Seienden und dem Sein die Differenz zum voraus anbringt. Zu dieser anscheinend einleuchtenden, aber auch schnell fertigen Erklärung wäre vieles zu sagen und noch mehr zu fragen, allem voran dieses: Woher kommt das «zwischen», in das die Differenz gleichsam eingeschoben werden soll?

Wir lassen Meinungen und Erklärungen fahren, beachten statt dessen folgendes: Überall und jederzeit finden wir das, was Differenz genannt wird, in der Sache des Denkens, im Seienden als solchem vor, so zweifelsfrei, daß wir diesen Befund gar nicht erst als solchen zur Kenntnis nehmen. Auch zwingt uns nichts, dies zu tun. Unserem Denken steht es frei, die Differenz unbedacht zu lassen oder sie eigens als solche zu bedenken. Aber diese Freiheit gilt nicht für alle Fälle. Unversehens kann der Fall eintreten, daß sich das Denken in die Frage gerufen findet: Was sagt denn dieses vielgenannte Sein? Zeigt sich hierbei das Sein sogleich als Sein des . . ., somit im Genitiv der Differenz, dann lautet die vorige Frage sachlicher: Was haltet ihr von der Differenz, wenn sowohl das Sein als auch das Seiende je auf ihre Weise *aus der Differenz her* erscheinen? Um dieser Frage zu genügen, müssen wir uns erst zur Differenz in ein sachgemäßes Gegenüber bringen. Dieses Gegenüber öffnet sich uns, wenn wir den Schritt zurück vollziehen. Denn durch die von ihm erbrachte Ent-Fernung gibt sich zuerst das Nahe als solches, kommt Nähe zum ersten Scheinen. Durch den Schritt zurück lassen wir die Sache des Denkens, Sein als Differenz, in ein Gegenüber frei, welches Gegenüber durchaus gegenstandslos bleiben kann.

Immer noch auf die Differenz blickend und sie doch schon durch den Schritt zurück in das zu-Denkende entlassend, können wir sagen: Sein des Seienden heißt: Sein, welches das Seiende ist. Das «ist» spricht hier transitiv, übergehend. Sein west hier in der Weise eines Überganges zum Seienden. Sein geht jedoch nicht, seinen Ort verlassend, zum Seienden hinüber, so als könnte Seiendes, zuvor ohne das Sein, von diesem erst angegangen werden. Sein geht über (das) hin, kommt entbergend über (das), was durch solche Überkommnis erst als von sich her Unverborgenes ankommt. Ankunft heißt: sich bergen in Unverborgenheit: also geborgen an-währen: Seiendes sein.

Sein zeigt sich als die entbergende Überkommnis. Seiendes als solches erscheint in der Weise der in die Unverborgenheit sich bergenden Ankunft.

Sein im Sinne der entbergenden Überkommnis und Seiendes als solches im Sinne der sich bergenden Ankunft wesen als die so Unterschiedenen aus dem Selben, dem Unter-Schied. Dieser vergibt erst und hält auseinander das Zwischen, worin

Überkommnis und Ankunft zueinander gehalten, auseinander-zueinander getragen sind. Die Differenz von Sein und Seiendem ist als der Unter-Schied von Überkommnis und Ankunft der *entbergend-bergende Austrag* beider. Im Austrag waltet Lichtung des sich verhüllend Verschließenden, welches Walten das Aus- und Zueinander von Überkommnis und Ankunft vergibt.

Indem wir versuchen, die Differenz als solche zu bedenken, bringen wir sie nicht zum Verschwinden, sondern folgen ihr in ihre Wesensherkunft. Unterwegs zu dieser denken wir den Austrag von Überkommnis und Ankunft. Es ist die um einen Schritt zurück sachlicher gedachte Sache des Denkens: Sein gedacht aus der Differenz.

Hier bedarf es freilich einer Zwischenbemerkung, die unser Reden von der Sache des Denkens angeht, eine Bemerkung, die immer neu unser Aufmerken verlangt. Sagen wir «das Sein», so gebrauchen wir das Wort in der weitesten und unbestimmtesten Allgemeinheit. Aber schon dann, wenn wir nur von einer Allgemeinheit sprechen, haben wir das Sein in einer ungemäßen Weise gedacht. Wir stellen das Sein in einer Weise vor, in der Es, das Sein, sich niemals gibt. Die Art, wie die Sache des Denkens, das Sein, sich verhält, bleibt ein einzigartiger Sachverhalt. Unsere geläufige Denkart kann ihn zunächst immer nur unzureichend verdeutlichen. Dies sei durch ein Beispiel versucht, wobei im voraus zu beachten ist, daß es für das Wesen des Seins nirgends im Seienden ein Beispiel gibt, vermutlich deshalb, weil das Wesen des Seins das Spiel selber ist.

Hegel erwähnt einmal zur Kennzeichnung der Allgemeinheit des Allgemeinen folgenden Fall: Jemand möchte in einem Geschäft Obst kaufen. Er verlangt Obst. Man reicht ihm Äpfel, Birnen, reicht ihm Pfirsiche, Kirschen, Trauben. Aber der Käufer weist das Dargereichte zurück. Er möchte um jeden Preis Obst haben. Nun *ist* aber doch das Dargebotene jedesmal Obst und dennoch stellt sich heraus: Obst gibt es nicht zu kaufen.

Unendlich unmöglicher bleibt es, «das Sein» als das Allgemeine zum jeweilig Seienden vorzustellen. Es gibt Sein nur je und je in dieser und jener geschicklichen Prägung: Φύσις, Λόγος, ῞Εν, ᾿Ιδέα, Ἐνέργεια, Substanzialität, Objektivität, Subjektivität, Wille, Wille zur Macht, Wille zum Willen. Aber dies Geschickliche gibt es nicht aufgereiht wie Äpfel, Birnen, Pfirsiche, aufgereiht auf dem Ladentisch des historischen Vorstellens.

134

Doch hörten wir nicht vom Sein in der geschichtlichen Ordnung und Folge des dialektischen Prozesses, den Hegel denkt? Gewiß. Aber das Sein gibt sich auch hier nur in dem Lichte, das sich für Hegels Denken gelichtet hat. Das will sagen: Wie es, das Sein, sich gibt, bestimmt sich je selbst aus der Weise, wie es sich lichtet. Diese Weise ist jedoch eine geschickliche, eine je epochale Prägung, die für uns als solche nur west, wenn wir sie in das ihr eigene Gewesen freilassen. In die Nähe des Geschicklichen gelangen wir nur durch die Jähe des Augenblickes eines Andenkens. Dies gilt auch für die Erfahrung der jeweiligen Prägung der Differenz von Sein und Seiendem, der eine jeweilige Auslegung des Seienden als solchen entspricht. Das Gesagte gilt vor allem auch für unseren Versuch, im Schritt zurück aus der Vergessenheit der Differenz als solcher an diese als den Austrag von entbergender Überkommnis und sich bergender Ankunft zu denken. Zwar bekundet sich einem genaueren Hinhören, daß wir in diesem Sagen vom Austrag bereits das Gewesene zum Wort kommen lassen, insofern wir an Entbergen und Bergen, an Übergang (Transzendenz) und an Ankunft (Anwesen) denken. Vielleicht kommt sogar durch diese Erörterung der Differenz von Sein und Seiendem in den Austrag als den Vorort ihres Wesens etwas Durchgängiges zum Vorschein, was das Geschick des Seins vom Anfang bis in seine Vollendung durchgeht. Doch bleibt es schwierig zu sagen, wie diese Durchgängigkeit zu denken sei, wenn sie weder ein Allgemeines ist, das für alle Fälle gilt, noch ein Gesetz, das die Notwendigkeit eines Prozesses im Sinne des Dialektischen sicherstellt.

Worauf es jetzt für unser Vorhaben allein ankommt, ist der Einblick in eine Möglichkeit, die Differenz als Austrag so zu denken, daß deutlicher wird, inwiefern die onto-theologische Verfassung der Metaphysik ihre Wesensherkunft im Austrag hat, der die Geschichte der Metaphysik beginnt, ihre Epochen durchwaltet, jedoch überall *als* der Austrag verborgen und so vergessen bleibt in einer selbst sich noch entziehenden Vergessenheit.

Um den genannten Einblick zu erleichtern, bedenken wir das Sein und in ihm die Differenz und in dieser den Austrag von jener Prägung des Seins her, durch die das Sein sich als Λόγος, als der Grund gelichtet hat. Das Sein zeigt sich in der entbergenden Überkommnis als das Vorliegenlassen des Ankommenden, als das Gründen in den mannigfaltigen Weisen des Her- und Vorbringens. Das Seiende als solches, die sich in die Unverborgenheit bergende Ankunft ist das Gegründete, das als Gegründetes und so als Erwirktes auf seine Weise gründet, nämlich wirkt, d. h. verursacht. Der Austrag von Gründendem und Gegründetem als solchem hält beide nicht nur auseinander, er hält sie im Zueinander. Die Auseinandergetragenen sind dergestalt in den Austrag verspannt, daß nicht nur Sein als Grund das Seiende gründet, sondern das Seiende seinerseits auf seine Weise das Sein gründet, es verursacht. Solches vermag das Seiende nur, insofern es die Fülle des Seins «ist»: als das Seiendste.

Hier gelangt unsere Besinnung in einen erregenden Zusammenhang. Sein west als Λόγος im Sinne des Grundes, des Vorliegenlassens. Derselbe Λόγος ist als Versammlung das Einende, das ῞Εν. Dieses ῞Εν jedoch ist zwiefältig: Einmal das Eine Einende im Sinne des überall Ersten und so Allgemeinsten und zugleich das Eine Einende im Sinne des Höchsten (Zeus). Der Λόγος versammelt gründend alles in das Allgemeine und versammelt begründend alles aus dem Einzigen. Daß derselbe Λόγος überdies die Wesensherkunft der Prägung des Sprachwesens in sich birgt und so die Weise des Sagens als eines logischen im weiteren Sinne bestimmt, sei nur beiläufig vermerkt.

Insofern Sein als Sein des Seienden, als die Differenz, als der

137

Austrag west, währt das Aus- und Zueinander von Gründen und Begründen, gründet Sein das Seiende, begründet das Seiende als das Seiendste das Sein. Eines überkommt das Andere, Eines kommt im Anderen an. Überkommnis und Ankunft erscheinen wechselweise ineinander im Widerschein. Von der Differenz her gesprochen, heißt dies: Der Austrag ist ein Kreisen, das Umeinanderkreisen von Sein und Seiendem.

Das Gründen selber erscheint innerhalb der Lichtung des Austrags als etwas, das *ist*, was somit selber, als Seiendes, die entsprechende Begründung durch Seiendes, d. h. die Verursachung und zwar die durch die höchste Ursache verlangt.

Einer der klassischen Belege für diesen Sachverhalt in der Geschichte der Metaphysik findet sich in einem kaum beachteten Text von Leibniz, welchen Text wir kurz «Die 24 Thesen der Metaphysik» nennen (Gerh. Phil VII, 289 ff.; vgl. dazu: Der Satz vom Grund, 1957, S. 51 f.).

Die Metaphysik entspricht dem Sein als Λόγος und ist demgemäß in ihrem Hauptzug überall Logik, aber Logik, die das Sein des Seienden denkt, demgemäß die vom Differenten der Differenz her bestimmte Logik: Onto-Theo-Logik.

Insofern die Metaphysik das Seiende als solches im Ganzen denkt, stellt sie das Seiende aus dem Hinblick auf das Differente der Differenz vor, ohne auf die Differenz als Differenz zu achten.

Das Differente zeigt sich als das Sein des Seienden im Allgemeinen und als das Sein des Seienden im Höchsten.

Weil Sein als Grund erscheint, ist das Seiende das Gegründete, das höchste Seiende aber das Begründende im Sinne der ersten Ursache. Denkt die Metaphysik das Seiende im Hinblick auf seinen jedem Seienden als solchem gemeinsamen Grund, dann ist sie Logik als Onto-Logik. Denkt die Metaphysik das Seiende als solches im Ganzen, d. h. im Hinblick auf das höchste, alles begründende Seiende, dann ist sie Logik als Theo-Logik.

Weil das Denken der Metaphysik in die als solche ungedachte Differenz eingelassen bleibt, ist die Metaphysik aus der einigenden Einheit des Austrags her einheitlich zumal Ontologie und Theologie.

Die onto-theologische Verfassung der Metaphysik entstammt dem Walten der Differenz, die Sein als Grund und Seiendes als gegründet-begründendes aus- und zueinanderhält, welches Aushalten der Austrag vollbringt.

Was so heißt, verweist unser Denken in den Bereich, den zu sagen die Leitworte der Metaphysik, Sein und Seiendes,

Grund – Gegründetes, nicht mehr genügen. Denn was diese Worte nennen, was die von ihnen geleitete Denkweise vorstellt, stammt als das Differente aus der Differenz. Deren Herkunft läßt sich nicht mehr im Gesichtskreis der Metaphysik denken.

Der Einblick in die onto-theologische Verfassung der Metaphysik zeigt einen möglichen Weg, die Frage: Wie kommt der Gott in die Philosophie? aus dem Wesen der Metaphysik zu beantworten.

Der Gott kommt in die Philosophie durch den Austrag, den wir zunächst als den Vorort des Wesens der Differenz von Sein und Seiendem denken. Die Differenz macht den Grundriß im Bau des Wesens der Metaphysik aus. Der Austrag ergibt und vergibt das Sein als her-vor-bringenden Grund, welcher Grund selbst aus dem von ihm Begründeten her der ihm gemäßen Begründung, d. h. der Verursachung durch die ursprünglichste Sache bedarf. Dies ist die Ursache als die Causa sui. So lautet der sachgerechte Name für den Gott in der Philosophie. Zu diesem Gott kann der Mensch weder beten, noch kann er ihm opfern. Vor der Causa sui kann der Mensch weder aus Scheu ins Knie fallen, noch kann er vor diesem Gott musizieren und tanzen.

Demgemäß ist das gott-lose Denken, das den Gott der Philosophie, den Gott als Causa sui preisgeben muß, dem göttlichen Gott vielleicht näher. Dies sagt hier nur: Es ist freier für ihn, als es die Onto-Theo-Logik wahrhaben möchte. Durch diese Bemerkung mag ein geringes Licht auf den Weg fallen, zu dem ein Denken unterwegs ist, das den Schritt zurück vollzieht, zurück aus der Metaphysik in das Wesen der Metaphysik, zurück aus der Vergessenheit der Differenz als solcher in das Geschick der sich entziehenden Verbergung des Austrags.

Niemand kann wissen, ob und wann und wo und wie dieser Schritt des Denkens zu einem eigentlichen (im Ereignis gebrauchten) Weg und Gang und Wegebau sich entfaltet. Es könnte sein, daß die Herrschaft der Metaphysik sich eher verfestigt und zwar in der Gestalt der modernen Technik und deren unabsehbaren rasenden Entwicklungen. Es könnte auch sein, daß alles, was sich auf dem Weg des Schrittes zurück ergibt, von der fortbestehenden Metaphysik auf ihre Weise als Ergebnis eines vorstellenden Denkens nur genützt und verarbeitet wird.

So bliebe der Schritt zurück selbst unvollzogen und der Weg, den er öffnet und weist, unbegangen.

Solche Überlegungen drängen sich leicht auf, aber sie haben kein Gewicht im Verhältnis zu einer ganz anderen Schwierigkeit, durch die der Schritt zurück hindurch muß.

Das Schwierige liegt in der Sprache. Unsere abendländischen Sprachen sind in je verschiedener Weise Sprachen des metaphysischen Denkens. Ob das Wesen der abendländischen Sprachen in sich nur metaphysisch und darum endgültig durch die Onto-Theo-Logik geprägt ist, oder ob diese Sprachen andere Möglichkeiten des Sagens und d. h. zugleich des sagenden Nichtsagens gewähren, muß offen bleiben. Oft genug hat sich uns während der Seminarübungen das Schwierige gezeigt, dem das denkende Sagen ausgesetzt bleibt. Das kleine Wort «ist», das überall in unserer Sprache spricht und vom Sein sagt, auch dort, wo es nicht eigens hervortritt, enthält – vom ἔστιν γάρ εἶναι des Parmenides an bis zum «ist» des spekulativen Satzes bei Hegel und bis zur Auflösung des «ist» in eine Setzung des Willens zur Macht bei Nietzsche – das ganze Geschick des Seins.

Der Blick in dieses Schwierige, das aus der Sprache kommt, sollte uns davor behüten, die Sprache des jetzt versuchten Denkens vorschnell in eine Terminologie umzumünzen und morgen schon vom Austrag zu reden, statt alle Anstrengung dem Durchdenken des Gesagten zu widmen. Denn das Gesagte wurde in einem Seminar gesagt. Ein Seminar ist, was das Wort andeutet, ein Ort und eine Gelegenheit, hier und dort einen Samen, ein Samenkorn des Nachdenkens auszustreuen, das irgendwann einmal auf seine Weise aufgehen mag und fruchten.

Zum Versuch, das Ding zu denken, vgl. *Vorträge und Aufsätze*, Neske, Pfullingen 1954, S. 163–181, 3. Auflage 1967, Teil II S. 37–55. Der Vortrag «Das Ding» wurde zum erstenmal innerhalb einer Vortragsreihe «Einblick in das, was ist» im Dezember 1949 zu Bremen und im Frühjahr 1950 auf Bühlerhöhe gehalten.

Zur Auslegung des Satzes des Parmenides vgl. a. a. O. S. 231 bis 256.

Zum Wesen der modernen Technik und der neuzeitlichen Wissenschaft vgl. a. a. O. S. 13–70.

Zur Bestimmung des Seins als Grund vgl. a. a. O. S. 207–229 und *Der Satz vom Grund*, Neske, Pfullingen 1957.

Zur Erörterung der Differenz vgl. *Was heißt denken?*, Niemeyer, Tübingen 1954 und *Zur Seinsfrage*, Klostermann, Frankfurt a. M. 1956.

Zur Auslegung der Metaphysik Hegels vgl. *Holzwege*, Klostermann, Frankfurt a. M. 1950, S. 105–192.

Erst im Zurückdenken aus der vorliegenden Schrift und den hier angeführten Veröffentlichungen wird der *Brief über den Humanismus* (1947), der überall nur andeutend spricht, ein möglicher Anstoß zu einer Auseinandersetzung der Sache des Denkens.

Designed by Robert Freese
Set in 10 point Bodoni Book
Composed, printed and bound by The Haddon Craftsmen, Inc.
HARPER & ROW, PUBLISHERS, INCORPORATED